NATALIA CINTRA, DAVID OWEN AND
PÍA RIGGIROZZI

DISPLACEMENT, HUMAN RIGHTS AND SEXUAL AND REPRODUCTIVE HEALTH

Conceptualizing Gender Protection Gaps in Latin America

BRISTOL
UNIVERSITY
PRESS

First published in Great Britain in 2023 by

Bristol University Press
University of Bristol
1–9 Old Park Hill
Bristol
BS2 8BB
UK
t: +44 (0)117 374 6645
e: bup-info@bristol.ac.uk

Details of international sales and distribution partners are available at
bristoluniversitypress.co.uk

British Library Cataloguing in Publication Data
A catalogue record for this book is available from the British Library

ISBN 978-1-5292-2279-1 hardcover
ISBN 978-1-5292-2280-7 ePub
ISBN 978-1-5292-2281-4 ePdf

Cover design: Dave Worth
Front cover image: Photograph by Bruna Curcio
Bristol University Press uses environmentally responsible print partners.
Printed and bound in Great Britain by CPI Group (UK) Ltd, Croydon, CR0 4YY

FSC
www.fsc.org
MIX
Paper | Supporting responsible forestry
FSC® C013604

We dedicate this book to all displaced women and the women who have supported us in our own journey across this project.

Contents

List of Figures and Tables

Figures

Tables

Acknowledgements

This book is a collective enterprise like no other. It is truly the result of the shared thinking and reflection of everyone involved in a bigger project, of which the book is part, titled 'Redressing Gendered Health Inequalities of Displaced Women and Girls in Central and South America' (ReGHID). ReGHID has brought together Zeni Lamy, at the Universidade Federal do Maranhão (Brazil); Maria Do Carmo Leal, at the Fiocruz Foundation, Rio de Janeiro (Brazil); Rita Bacuri at the Fiocruz Foundation, Manaus (Brazil); Monica Linares and Henry Garcia from FLACSO El Salvador, Jovana Ocampo Cañas and Jhon Sebastian Patiño Rueda at the Universidad de los Andes (Colombia); the International Organization for Migration (IOM) Honduras and El Salvador; Jean Grugel and Rodrigo Moreno Serra at the University of York, and Sarah Neal, Amos Channon and Sarahí Rueda at the University of Southampton in the UK, and many other people across and beyond those institutions. We thank them all for their intellectual and personal generosity and support, for their careful, insightful and collaborative work, and fundamentally for sharing a passionate commitment to defend the human rights of refugee and migrant women and girls, and redress injustices and inequalities in health and in many aspects of their lives for being women and being displaced – all of which define the aim of this book.

We are specially indebted to Adriana Rodriguez, a migrant from Central America living in Manaus, and a committed and dedicated member of the community helping many other migrants in Brazil. Adriana together with ReGHID co-investigators in Brazil facilitated access, online and in person, to shelters and to the many migrant women and girls we interviewed for this project in Manaus and Boa Vista. We are particularly grateful to Zeni Lamy at Universidade Federal do Maranhão who co-designed the methodology for fieldwork and access to shelters, and to Valeria Ottonelli at Università di Genova, who provided essential feedback to us which enriched this book and the overall project. We were lucky and thankful to have financial support from the Economic and Social Research Council (ESRC) (grant number ES/T00441X/1), for all activities related to ReGHID.

Others whose thought-provoking thinking, and insightful comments greatly helped in improving the clarity of this book are Alex Aleinikoff, Rebecca Hamlin, Gloria Zuccarelli and Jean Grugel, who read draft and chapters, as well as Marcia Vera Espinosa and Leiza Brumat, who discussed this and related work in panels at conferences. We also appreciate the incessant administrative, editorial and human support provided by Claudia Drake.

But our biggest debt of gratitude goes to the many Venezuelan migrant women and girls we have met over the course of this project. They shared with us the most intimate reasons for fleeing and their challenging experiences while in displacement and in places of settlement, and how directly or indirectly risks and vulnerabilities affected their health, particularly undermining the right to health, and their specific sexual and reproductive health needs and rights. We have been touched by the difficult situations they face in their everyday lives, as much as by their strength and determination despite that. We also learned with them about how respect and acceptance of migrants are far too often tied to arbitrary understandings of deservingness and responsibility. We hope that this book contributes to improving their circumstances now and in the years to come.

Outside the academic work, the unreserved love and support of our families have been, once again, an essential emotional anchor for which Natalia, David and Pía are eternally thankful.

Note on Figure 4.2

Figure 4.2 has been published in a font size smaller than our house style. To see a full-sized version of this figure, please visit https://bristoluniversitypress.co.uk/displacement-human-rights-and-sexual-and-reproductive-health.

Introduction

It is September 2020 and Grecia, a 35-year-old Venezuelan woman who is eight months pregnant, and her four children aged 2, 6, 10 and 13 are facing severe hunger and other deprivations. She is unemployed, a single mother with no support, and confronted by a maternal health system in collapse:

> 'I spent five months thinking and thinking, my children were crying of hunger, they had no clothes, the oldest wanted to study but it was all impossible facing the pandemic [of COVID-19] … on 1st September, at 3am, I took my children and started to walk [to Brazil] … we came all the way by foot.' (Boa Vista, 28 September 2021)

The border between Venezuela and Brazil is closed from March 2020 for over a year. Due to COVID-19 the entry of foreigners is prohibited; they have no choice but to walk and cross by *trocha*: irregular and unofficial (and unsafe) pathways of crossing. Grecia, like many other women, walked for days. She arrives at the border town of Pacaraima in Brazilian state of Roraima, where she is escorted by the Brazilian Army to a triage centre, where the estimated 700 Venezuelans who enter each day are profiled and given a place to sleep:

> 'When the border officers arrived, they gave us wristbands and took us to a shelter … I did not know that we had to leave in the morning, taking the luggage with us, to the streets. The shelter was only to sleep, overnight … and for the time it took to get all our documents … once we had the documents, mine and

of my children, they sent us to another shelter, for two weeks … then to Boa Vista.'

Grecia spends over 4 weeks with no information on healthcare or prenatal health checks. Her pregnancy is coming to term, and she has been exposed to very challenging circumstances before, during and after fleeing. She's tired and the uncertainty, particularly relating to whom she would leave the children with at the time of birth, in a foreign country, is creating too much anxiety. She cannot find emotional support or appropriate information in response to her needs. It is only after arrival at the city of Boa Vista that someone in the new shelter suggests that she goes to a health unit for her pregnancy checks. She is entitled to that by law. But she has to wait because "we arrived on a Friday to the shelter, and they don't work on Saturdays and Sundays".

Since 2016 a new corridor of forced migration has been opened up by the mass displacement of Venezuelans to neighbouring countries fleeing hunger, poverty, violence and the collapse of the welfare state. In 2016, 200,000 Venezuelans left the country, double the average rate per year since 1999. By 2023, the number of displaced Venezuelans grew to 7 million, fleeing the spiralling economic collapse that left basic food and medicine increasingly out of reach for most of the Venezuelan population. The current exodus of Venezuelans has generated the largest migration crisis of its kind in recent Latin American history.

While every person fleeing represents an individual story, often of constrained choices and injustices before and during displacements, and in places of abode, many of those stories have revealed a distinctively gendered feature of the Venezuelan displacement: an exodus of thousands of pregnant women, fleeing for reasons of practical necessity including fear of losing their babies or their own lives if they remained to give birth in their own country. According to Amnesty International (2018), between 2015 and 2016, maternal mortality increased by 65 per cent in Venezuela, a regression of 25 years due to the lack of medicines such as anticoagulants, scar healing cream, painkillers, antibiotics, antiseptics; the lack of basic medical tools and equipment, such as scalpels, needles and gloves; and the ever-falling number of medical personnel willing to work with no equipment and without pay.

This context prompted many women to flee, as we analyse in this book, because they wanted to secure for themselves and their families better medical care, better opportunities for education for their children, and the chance to live a dignified life. This is a way in which forced migration is gendered. Social expectations may place women in the household and in society as the first ones to take care of health needs, seek medical help and be sensitive to the health needs of their families. But it is also gendered because these women have a special concern for their own sexual and reproductive health. It is not that Venezuelan women flee alone or accompanied, and engage in perilous journeys *despite* their pregnancy, ill-health or care responsibilities of small children or elderly relatives, rather they migrate *because* of their personal circumstance and care responsibilities, exercising their agency and conveying their awareness that what they are fighting for is not mere survival, but reclaiming their human rights and entitlements, including the right to sexual and reproductive health.

Many forced migrants flee poverty and dangerous conditions that affect their health and access to healthcare. Exposure to ill-health and disease are consequently significant, and often a reason to leave. The journeys are also a continuum of poverty and precarity as smuggled and trafficked persons are exposed to all sorts of dangers, risks of sexual assault, burglary, abuse, exposure to heat, cold or injury, hunger and dehydration, the fears and dangers of being attacked by wild animals, suffocation in containers, or the risk of drowning. Scholarship on gendered risk and insecurities during migration highlights the physical risks and forms of violence experienced by women during migratory journeys and after border crossing (Gerard and Pickering 2014; Freedman 2016; 2017). Sahraoui and Tyszler (2021) also explore how on arrival many women and girls might be subject to arbitrary management of documentation and border control, vigilance and militarization. In relation to determinants of physical and mental health of forcibly displaced people, refugees and protection seekers, Kneebone (2019) explores the continued disadvantages, poverty and dependences that migrants face during dangerous journeys and in places of arrival, and how ambivalent implementation of international frameworks regarding health rights discriminate against irregular migrants.

In many different ways, displaced populations are at risk and exposed to unique and complex sets of political, economic, ethnic-based and gendered disparities that undermine their health needs and rights, and that require attention both on arrival and throughout the process of settlement.

Olga travelled from Venezuela to Brazil, with her two daughters aged 14 and 15, walking for three days from 22 to 25 December 2020 when they arrived in Manaus. As she recalls:

> 'We left on the 22nd in the afternoon and spent the night on the road. We arrived the next day at the border, at two in the afternoon and to Boa Vista on the 24th. That night we stayed in the street to take a bus that finally took us to Manaus … we had money for that bus but others walk for five days, asking for rides and hitchhiking … on the trails there were tigers, there were pumas. That was my great fear. There were thugs who robbed people, another fear. But I was ready, for my children I was ready to face that … ready for whatever happened, entrusted to God … at some point we had to climb a mountain, on that mountain there were many cliffs, many holes. And one of my daughters slipped and hung there. She grabbed a branch because she was going into the void. The *trochero* [smuggler]

> helped her to climb back on track and continue.' (Manaus, 8 June 2021)

As forcibly displaced women such as Grecia and Olga cross borders, they continue to experience increased disadvantages due to their gender, including discrimination, sexual violence and socioeconomic exploitation. Their vulnerability is heightened by their lack (or loss) of documentation, of social networks, and of sources of income. These, typically, limit access to public services, including health and social services, as well as job opportunities, information, nutrition, education, and restrict their integration into society. Particularly in border areas, situations of pre-existing poverty and uneven development can significantly increase (forced) migrants' exposure to further poverty, harms and risks. The COVID-19 pandemic has compounded these disadvantages.

Because of modalities of travelling and crossing, and their status, displaced people often have their rights, including their right to health, curtailed or neglected. Furthermore, the risks taken, and needs of, displaced people are not gender neutral, and systems of protection should respond to the gendered needs and rights of migrants and refugees. Yet rather than responding to these health needs in a gender-responsive manner, many receiving countries exhibit ambiguities in governance and avoidance of responsibility, even criminalizing or stigmatizing displaced women and reproducing gender inequalities as a consequence.

This book addresses the intersection of gender, forced migration and health. Using the case of displaced women from Venezuela, it focuses on how current protection regimes fail displaced women and what is needed for protection to be responsive to the gendered character of forced migration. We adopt a gender and rights lens to address threats to the sexual and reproductive health of female forced migrants as a central issue for any adequately gender-sensitive system of protection. First, exposure to such threats may be the basis on which the decision to flee is made – and hence a gender-responsive system of protection must recognize such exposure as grounding the entitlement to protection. Second, the circumstances and conditions of flight may themselves generate threats to the sexual and reproductive health of women – and hence a gender-responsive system of protection must recognize the gendered character of 'safe passage' and the ways in which this can be supported or undermined by the policies of the states to whom displaced women are fleeing. Third, the conditions of reception of female fleers in states of first refuge and of settlement in hosting states may expose these women to significant risks to their sexual and reproductive health, whether in terms of sexual violence and exploitation arising from their social position as displaced women or in terms of lack of access of sexual and reproductive health rights relating to their circumstances as migrants with particular legal or social statuses.

In this book, we address the gaps – conceptual, legal, practical – in the regimes of protection available to displaced women, and the challenges that they face, in order to show how the failure to conceive and enact a gender-sensitive regime of protection is itself a threat to the sexual and reproductive health of women. To do so requires that we engage with a range of literatures addressing issues of migration, gender and health from the perspectives of political theory, socio-legal studies, migration studies, and governance studies.

The most straightforward way to think about the form of the analysis and argument that we attempt to provide in this book in that it aims to elucidate the gap between what displaced women like Grecia and Olga are entitled to as displaced women and the conditions that they actually experience, to analyse the production of this condition, and to elaborate what would be needed to overcome this gap. This demands a layered approach to analysis. Thus we begin by sketching out their entitlements by offering an analysis of gender, forced migration, and the human right to health as instantiated in international and regional legal instruments and, to a lesser extent, governance structures. We then propose a conceptual and normative framework that can disclose the ways in which the disjuncture between promise and actuality is produced through conceptual, legal, and practical gaps in the regimes of protection, before finally articulating what a robust ethics of forced displacement that is responsive to the gendered character of such displacement and its implications for health and health rights would entail.

The initial problem we identify concerns the way in which the flight of such women is ethically conceptualized and legally categorized through the refugee/migrant binary. First, the flight of Venezuelan women does not fit easily with current conceptualizations of refugeehood and points to the limitations in form and substance of current operative determinations of who is a refugee. Second, this brings into play a distinction between refugees and migrants that allows states considerable capacity for differentiating between different groups of forced migrants and for instituting hierarchies of protection and access to rights. To address this conceptual gap, we argue for an ethics of forced displacement built around the concept of the necessary fleer (Aleinikoff and Zamore 2019). We use this framework to assess substantive protection gaps in the responses across Latin America, focusing on Brazil and Colombia, to displaced Venezuelan women and girls. Our purpose here is to show how states, and a region, characterized by liberal and progressive principles of protection adopt policies that, in practice, serve to differentiate between displaced women and construct a variety of obstacles to gender-sensitive forms of protection that expose displaced women to threats to their sexual and reproductive health. This analysis is extended by taking up the perspective of the displaced women themselves and their accounts of the challenges that they confront in gaining access to protection and health services. We show how state migration/protection policies affect access to health rights and the determinants of sexual and reproductive health.[1]

This layered analysis of the gaps in how protection is conceived and enacted, and their effects on displaced women, leads us finally to articulate an ethics of forced displacement that can be sensitive to the gendered character of such movement and to the central role that sexual and reproductive health has in any adequate regime of protection. We develop an account of protection based on the human right to health in contexts of displacement and propose a gendered account of 'forced displacement' beyond the continuum of 'migrant–refugee' to highlight the specificities of health as driver of (forced) migration and of migration statuses as a determinant of gendered health inequalities affecting displaced women and girls. In doing so the book also discusses key ethical and legal issues, recognizing that any efforts to break cycles of deprivation and exclusion affecting displaced women and girls should privilege fulfilment of the right to health as a determinant of development and social agency.

The urgency of this task is driven by the recognition that the context and reasons for displacement, and the modality of journeys and settlement condition the experience and outcomes of sexual and reproductive health (SRH) of migrant women and girls as well as their wellbeing and personal autonomy. Yet current gaps in conceptualizations and practices of protection leave many displaced women and girls unprotected even with respect to such basic health rights as SRH rights. Identifying and addressing these gaps will, we hope, expand policy horizons by proposing a framework within which a just practice of protection can be produced.

Our approach: the dignity of displaced women and girls

The book aims to provide analytical and normative frameworks for addressing gendered inequalities in relation to displacement and systems of protection that respect and make sense of the testimony of Venezuelan women and girls who have fled to Brazil and Colombia, for whom gendered drivers of displacement have been significant, and yet lack protection of their general rights and still need to secure the conditions for decent sexual and reproductive health. The normative core of our work is a commitment to the dignity of these women and girls, and it will help to clarify what we mean by this.

Dignity is a complex phenomenon that, in its widest construal, encompasses a normative status, a practical relation to oneself, and a mode of conduct and comportment. Although historically dignity has been seen as legitimately differentiated in hierarchical terms (the dignity of the monarch being distinct from the dignity of their subjects, for example, who were also distinguished by rank), moral dignity is now identified as a single status of moral equality ascribed to all human beings and given clear legal expression as universal human rights. More colloquially, as Jeremy Waldron (2012: 5) puts it nicely:

> A person's dignity is not just some Kantian aura. It is their social standing, the fundamentals of basic reputation that entitle them to be treated as equals in the ordinary operation of society. Their dignity is something they can rely on – in the best case implicitly and without fuss, as they live their lives, go about their business, and raise their families.

That at least is the ideal – and this sense of dignity as a normative status protected by law and respected by one's fellows is central to our contemporary use of the concept. In the case of those who have been forcibly displaced such as the women and girls we engage in this book, this everyday colloquial sense of dignity is not something they can rely on. On the contrary, the lived experience of the loss of this everyday dignity is integral to their becoming displaced and to the experience of displacement.

To understand this experience, however, it will be helpful to distinguish two different ways in which dignity can fail to be recognized. On the one hand, dignity can be denied by the failure to observe rights, for example, the failure to protect human rights. Yet although such actions and omissions fail to respect a person's (or group's) dignity, they do not thereby *target* their dignity, that is to say that they are not expressively focused on rejecting their claim to dignity in the way that actions such as degradation, contempt, insult do. These actions are called 'dignitary harms' precisely because they are focused on rejecting a person's (or group's) entitlement to dignity as an equal status. We might say that the former denies the dignity *of* one's person as a bearer of equal status expressed in terms of human rights; the latter rejects the dignity *in* one's person that grounds one's entitlement to enjoy equal status.

It is, of course, both true and important that a breach of the rights to which I am entitled as part of my dignity as an equal rights-bearer may be expressed in a way that also constitutes a dignitary harm. The same act may comprise both injury and insult. Think for example of sexual assault with respect to women and girls which both denies their right to bodily security and does so in a way that denigrates the equal standing of women and girls by treating them as objects available for the expression of male sexual desire. It is also true that some dignitary harms may also be breaches of rights; think, for example, of misogynistic defamation and hate speech which express the denial of the entitlement of women to equal status with men and do so in a way that wrongs women by making them liable to harms simply in virtue of being women. In these cases, insult is injury. But it remains important to distinguish analytically between the two types of failure to acknowledge a person's (or group's) dignity.

The significance of this point can be brought out by distinguishing what Michael Rosen calls 'respect as observance' and 'respect as respectfulness'. The former denotes my recognition of the dignity *of* your person in observing your rights. The latter refers to an attitude with which I interact with you. Thus, we may say that I acknowledge the dignity *in* your person by engaging respectfully with you as an equal.

The salience of the examples of sexual assault and misogynistic hate speech is to highlight that recognition of the dignity of women and girls requires both 'respect as observance' and 'respect as respectfulness' – and while the former may seem more immediately serious in contexts of protection, the latter may be more fundamental to creating and sustaining the commitment to gender equality that underpins the claim to equal rights. This relationship between the two dimensions of recognizing dignity is tragically illustrated by the fact that, as Rosen (2012: 97) notes:

> One of the features that have characterised many of the most violent and destructive acts of the twentieth century has been the humiliation and symbolic degradation of their victims. … It seems to be a fact about human nature that human beings are able more easily to engage in the most violent behaviour towards one another if at the same time they expressively deny the humanity of their victims.

As the moral disasters of the past century illustrate all too sharply, 'respect as respectfulness' is integral to the conditions of maintaining 'respect as observance' (see also Owen 2021).

Taking the dignity of displaced women and girls seriously thus means, from a normative standpoint, being alert to the ways in which regimes of protection enact (or fail to enact) both 'respect as observance' and 'respect as respectfulness', and the implications and consequences of these modes of protection. This can manifest itself as the level of a system of protection as a whole by, for example, treating displaced women and girls as rights-bearers who are subject *to* protection (respect as observance) but failing to engage with them as subjects *of* protection who are entitled to voice concerning how they are governed by the regime of protection (respect as respectfulness). It can also exhibit itself in respect of specific elements of protection. Thus, for example, access to SRH services may be an observed right for only some displaced women and girls because only some are recognized as falling under a given regime of protection (respect as observance), while even those whose entitlement is legally secure may or may not have effective access because of how they are treated by the health services (respect as respectfulness). Our orientation to the conditions confronted by displaced women and girls is thus concerned with both of these dimensions of acknowledging their dignity, and this normative orientation also guides the methodological commitment of our research to adopting a rights-based approach to the nexus of forced migration, gender, and health combined with taking the voices of displaced women and girls seriously.

Grounding the research in times of COVID-19

The analysis offered in this book was supported by primary and secondary data collected and analysed in the context of the ESRC GCRF-funded project 'Redressing Gendered Health Inequalities of Displaced Women and Girls in contexts of Protracted Crisis in Central and South America' – ReGHID. We embarked on this project with the goal of listening to the women and girls in order to reconstruct (through interviews and field observation) their experience as forcibly displaced migrants. Interviews and field trips to the camps and to the places where they settle in Brazil, and several discussions with other academics, particularly colleagues in the ReGHID project, both in Brazil and in Colombia, helped us to understand the everyday gendered challenges displaced women and adolescent girls face in relation to their sexual and reproductive health as well as in relation to shelters and the healthcare system.

We conducted fieldwork during 2020–2022. We planned to start interviews in person with Venezuelan displaced women in early 2020. Yet, as the COVID-19 pandemic hit, and Brazil became the epicentre of the health crisis in South America, our plans for travelling came to a halt. Brazil closed the borders to international travel, and to all migrants. While for many fleers of necessity this meant entering the country via alternative, irregular routes, by *trocha*, for us it meant finding alternative yet COVID-secure forms of reaching out to those displaced women and girls. We managed to do so with the help and support of co-investigators at the Federal University of Maranhão and Fiocruz in Manaus, and fundamentally with the help and support on the ground of a volunteer, Adriana, a migrant herself, working with migrant women in shelters, who acted as point of contact for all women and adolescent girls interviewed remotely, using Microsoft Teams. Adriana was provided with a dedicated mobile phone which we used exclusively for the interviews. We conducted interviews in Spanish with 75 displaced women aged 20–49 and adolescent girls aged 15–19 in Boa Vista and Pacaraima, where most Venezuelan migrants arrive when entering Brazil, and in Manaus, the second most common city of settlement. We also conducted online interviews with 35 key informants from the International Organization for Migration (IOM), the United Nations High Commissioner for Refugees (UNHCR), the United Nations Population Fund (UNFPA) and the United Nations Programme on HIV/AIDS (UNAIDS), and government agencies working with migrant women on the ground.

This was an incredible experience, not least because it proved how much these women and girls needed a space to talk, to express their concerns and hopes as well as to be heard and to become visible. They were incredibly frank and open to talking about their experiences, their perceptions of vulnerability and risks they faced, and the barriers to healthcare and protection in border areas and once they were settled. By May 2022, travel to Brazil was possible once again, and two of us travelled to Manaus and Boa Vista to engage in a further round of field research. We also had the opportunity to conduct face-to-face interviews with shelter coordinators, including military personnel and representatives from IOM and UNFPA, which were more informal and not transcribed. In addition, we conducted field observation, wrote field notes, and gathered visual documentary material. Finally, we also travelled to Bogotá around that time to meet co-investigators and discuss findings. Our research observed fully the appropriate ethical guidelines set out for research by the UK lead researcher institution, including the duty of researchers to do no harm. All names of interviewees have been changed to preserve anonymity.

Outline of the book

To develop our analysis, the book is divided into five chapters. Chapter 1 explores what feminization means in terms of flows and characteristics of displacement, including reasons for fleeing and experiences in displacement. The implications of this chapter are significant for how we situate the gendered causes and consequences of forced displacement. But it also brings to the fore the importance of gender-responsive protection to redress gendered inequalities and migration injustices. The chapter develops a rights-based framework that helps to analyse not only the nexus between displacement, gender and health, but also how responsibilities ought to be delivered in support of those needs and rights. We test these claims in the case of Latin America, with particular focus on the emergent corridor of migration from Venezuela to Colombia and to Brazil.

Chapter 2 explores the distinction between 'migrants' and 'refugees' in legal and political discourse as a way of differentially allocating responsibility for, and forms of protection of, different groups of 'people on the move'. It raises two issues concerning this distinction. The first addresses how it is itself gendered, that is, the ways in which it discriminates between drivers of migration to privilege some types of forced displacement over others in ways that have differential impacts on male and female movers. The second highlights its general inadequacy in capturing ethically salient features of movement. We argue that this conceptual schema is inadequate to the diverse and multifaceted character of transnational movement and use the examples of the current Venezuelan displacement crisis as lens to draw out the limitations of this schema for a political ethics of protection in displacement. Chapter 3 contextualizes the movement–health nexus in order to disclose gendered responsibility and protection gaps. It charts the relevant international and regional human rights instruments to analyse the norms that regulate and guide national and international institutions regarding the international protection of migrants and refugees. Chapter 4 refocuses attention on displaced women and girls as necessary fleers in order to detail the ways in which such displacement shapes their sexual and reproductive health. It contextualizes this discussion within the framework of the human right to health and aims to articulate the rights to which displaced women and girls are entitled and the terms on which they can exercise these rights as requirements of dignity. It then analyses whether existing protection systems at regional and national levels are implemented in the cases of Colombia and Brazil in responding to Venezuelan female migrants. The chapter addresses gendered needs regarding the SRH of women and the responsibilities of states to provide protection and evaluates implementation across the range of refugee and migrant statuses in terms of whether they address the protection needs of female mobile population and their rights relating to SRH. A focused discussion is offered regarding whether and how conceptual and implementation gaps translate into 'protection' gaps in relation to the migration and health nexus in the region. This analysis highlights the lack of adequate infrastructures and policies needed to break cycles of deprivation and exclusion specifically affecting displaced women and girls. The chapter highlights the inadequacy of protection frameworks for displaced women and the relationship of this protection gap to the ways in which responsibility for displaced women is allocated. Chapter 5 returns to the philosophical argument developed in Chapter 2 and asks who is responsible for ensuring the protection of the SRH rights of displaced women. The chapter draws out the implications of the reconceptualization of displaced persons as necessary fleers for the distribution of responsibility and the forms of protection owed to them. In concluding, we draw attention to the context of Latin America, the 'mixed' nature of migration flows from Venezuela, and the reproduction of protection gaps despite progressive laws and rhetoric regarding migrants and refugees. The conclusion offers a research agenda based on the salience of this analysis for other regions in which forced displacement of women and girls is a significant issue as well the challenges that addressing the identified responsibility and protection gaps poses to the various agents on whom the duty of protection lies.

ONE

The Gendered Character of Forced Migration

The current global estimate of forcibly displaced persons is 89.3 million (53.2 million are internally displaced, 27.1 million are refugees, 4.6 million are asylum seekers), a population that has been increasing consistently over the last decade. In 2020, prior to the outbreak of the war in Ukraine, approximately 5 million of those categorized as refugees were women between the ages of 12 and 59; a number that will have risen significantly given the demographics of flight from Ukraine.[1] This global data should draw two points to our attention. First, the issue of forcibly displaced persons is a significant and growing issue. It is, moreover, likely to keep growing given global challenges arising from wars, climate change, food insecurities, and gender-based violence that interact with each other and are not likely to decline any time soon. Second, there has been a 'feminization' of forced migration with women and girls making up a large, and increasingly visible, percentage of forced migrants, with many travelling without male spouses or relatives, but also, and more importantly, becoming displaced for gender-related reasons and exposed to gender-related risks in transit and in settlement.

Importantly, almost all conditions surrounding displacement processes exacerbate health vulnerabilities and risk behaviours among women and girls. There is compelling evidence that risks and vulnerabilities faced by displaced women and adolescent girls seriously affect their health, particularly undermining the right to health, and their specific SRH needs and rights (Starrs et al 2018; Wickramage and Annunziata 2018). There is also significant social scientific literature on migration as a determinant of ill-health within displaced populations and on the challenges in displacement, including risks of rape, trafficking, sexual assault, abuse and other risks related to poverty, stigma, discrimination, social exclusion, language, cultural differences and socio-cultural norms, as well as legal status (Valdez et al 2015; Barot 2017; Wolf 2020). Much of this literature has built on studies of conflict-related displacement in places such as Afghanistan, Yemen, Syria, South Sudan and Colombia, and has identified evidence linking displacement with health vulnerabilities of female forced migrants particularly exposed to risks of exploitation, sexual violence, and risky sexual behaviour for (economic) survival leading to increasing numbers of unwanted pregnancies, HIV and sexually transmitted infections (STIs), maternal death and precarity in general (Whelan and Blogg 2007; UNFPA 2009; Freedman 2016, 2017; PAHO 2019a). These contributions, together with some interventions to address these issues (CARE/ODI 2014; UN Women 2016) have paved the way for a more effective theorization of the intersections between migration, gender and health. Some key work in the field has been done addressing migrants and refugees from Southeast Asia and Sub-Saharan Africa travelling to Europe and Australia (for instance, Temin et al 2013; Chant et al 2017; Freedman 2017), but the experiences and SRH needs of those who move, particularly female forced migrants, within South-South corridors remain largely overlooked (PAHO 2019b).

Our focus is addressing the forced migration, gender, and health nexus in a South-South context by focusing on the case of Venezuela and the flight of around 20 per cent of its population, approximately 50 per cent of such fleers being women and girls, primarily to neighbouring states with Colombia and Brazil being two primary destinations. The Venezuelan case, however, also draws particular attention to a key issue for the protection of displaced persons, namely, the role of legal and administrative categories in shaping access to, for example, SRH rights. Thus, exceptionally, when it comes to the UNHCR data on Venezuela, we find three categories. In the most recent data on Venezuelans, it was recorded that there are 199,202 refugees under the UNHCR mandate, 971,131 asylum seekers, and 4,406,409 in the novel category of 'Venezuelans displaced abroad'.[2] The reasons for the invention of this novel category and its significance is a topic that we will explore, but for now we may note that the fact that more than 4 million Venezuelans are not identified as refugees or asylum seekers raises a query concerning the adequacy and effectiveness of the international refugee regime with respect to the protection of those forcibly displaced from their home countries.

In this chapter, we provide the contexts for our enquiry by addressing the nexus between forced migration and gender before introducing the issue of health and the right to health. We turn then to sketch out the theorization of displacement as a social determinant of health, before concluding by contextualizing the Venezuelan situation which is our focus in this work.

Forced migration, gender and UNHCR

The nexus of forced migration and gender raises a set of specific issues concerning reasons of flight, safe passage and secure settlement that cannot be adequately addressed by appeal to the abstract figure of 'the refugee', all too often encoded as male (Zuccarelli 2022). Many forced migrants flee conditions of poverty, conflict, poor health systems and high burdens of disease with migration perceived as the only viable alternative to deprivation and suffering. Yet the conditions surrounding migration, and forced migration in particular, increase gender inequalities and expose migrant women and girls to different and typically greater risks, and often poorer outcomes, than their male counterparts. For many women and girls, migration is a means by which they flee situations that are already detrimental to their wellbeing and dignity, frequently related to sexual and gender-based violence, but the process of migration also exposes women to gendered risks in transit and in settlement. As UNHCR (2016: 8) notes: 'Displacement often serves to exacerbate pre-existing forms of SGBV [sexual and gender-based violence], including domestic violence, sexual assault, forced and early marriage, torture, sexual harassment, human trafficking, forced sex work, female genital mutilation and homophobic violence.'

The point was officially recognized by UNHCR in the 1990s with issuance of the *Policy on Refugee Women* (1990), *Guidelines on the Protection of Refugee Women* (1991), and *Sexual Violence Against Refugees: Guidelines on Prevention and Response* (1995) although the backstory to these developments arguably goes back as far as 1975 with increasingly concerted efforts between 1985 and 1990 (also Martin 2010: 104–21). A particular concern was that since 'gender' was not included as a ground on which refugee status could be claimed, women in a range of threatening situations that make flight a compelling practical option, and perhaps the best or only viable option, would be unable to secure protection as refugees. Women who are subject to domestic abuse or transgress their society's gender codes, and are not able to get (or are denied) protection by their state; women who suffer severe sexual discrimination, particularly when enacted or facilitated by public agencies or officials; women who are de facto targets of military attacks; women who are victimized because of the political actions of a male relative – in all these cases, the claim to refugee status was potentially problematic and it is this situation which the 1991 *Guidelines on the Protection of Refugee Women* aimed to address (Martin 2010: 116–117).

Through the 1990s UNHCR increasingly shifted from a woman-based approach to a focus on gender analysis and gender equality, developing a strategy for mainstreaming gender equality into its protection programmes, while from the early 2000s, UNHCR introduced age as an additional focus in order to develop 'a strategy to promote gender equality and respect for women's rights and child rights in order to enhance the protection of refugees, rather than as a goal in itself' (UNHCR 2005: 3). This shift was, in part, a response to the 2001 review of a decade of implementation of the *Guidelines* (1991) which, as Freedman (2010: 598–99) notes,

> concluded that the Guidelines had succeeded in raising awareness among UNHCR staff and partners of women's specific needs and interests, but that overall the implementation of the Guidelines was 'uneven and incomplete, occurring on an ad hoc basis in certain sites rather than in a globally consistent and systematic way'. … A consultation exercise that the UNHCR organized with some refugee women came to similar conclusions that, despite progress in some areas, women refugees often still lacked access to food and other basic resources, and that they were not adequately protected against sexual and gender-based violence.

Consultations with refugee women also led UNHCR in 2001 to announce five commitments to refugee women in order to advance their rights and improve their protection, addressing: 1) Meaningful participation; 2) Individual registration and documentation; 3) Food and core relief items; 4) Economic empowerment; 5) Sexual and gender-based violence; and to release a year later the report *UNHCR Policy on Refugee Women and Guidelines on Their Protection: An Assessment of Ten Years of Implementation* (Women's Refugee Commission 2002). These were very positive steps in the recognition of refugee women's rights. Yet, over a decade and a half later, a review of progress highlighted significant challenges remaining in relation to each commitment:

Meaningful participation: 'Despite the notable progress, numerous operations highlight difficulties in ensuring that women play a meaningful role in leadership and management structures. Among the largest obstacles to participation are the socio-cultural norms that enforce restrictive gender roles. Also hindering women's participation … are high illiteracy rates, language barriers and domestic responsibilities. The 2011 UNHCR dialogues with persons of concern outlined several additional challenges faced by women. These include being marginalized by men in their families and communities; tokenistic inclusion; negative stereotyping of refugee women; and lack of access to childcare, transportation and compensation for lost income' (UNHCR 2016: 5).

Individual registration and documentation: 'Women and girls face numerous challenges in gaining access to individual registration, documentation and refugee status determination (RSD) procedures, threatening their ability to avail of rights and services. Among the difficulties highlighted … was the length of time registration can take … the lack of identity documents leads to unemployment, exploitation and harassment, besides making it difficult to obtain food, shelter, health care and social services. … Lack of documentation can mean denial of legal redress, creating an environment of impunity. Even in countries where identity documentation is provided, it is not always accepted by local authorities. In urban areas, lack of documentation can lead to arrest and detention. These challenges are particularly significant for female-headed households as they can give rise to a heightened risk of exploitation and abuse' (UNHCR 2016: 6).

Food and core relief items: 'The long distances women have to travel to distribution centres and/or extended waiting periods pose various risks. Women interviewed in one operation say they feel unsafe walking long distances in the dark, especially in areas with no street lighting, and that they are constantly worried about their children. They also speak of the lack of crowd management in distribution situations – similar to that witnessed first-hand at the height of recent refugee crises. … Budget cuts have also had a serious impact on food and CRI [core relief items] distribution. Concerns have been raised about the lack of food diversity and its effect on children's health, while almost all operations that report providing sanitary materials state that they have had to reduce distribution. In some operations, only persons with specific needs are provided with sanitary materials, leaving out large numbers of women and girls' (UNHCR 2016: 7).

Economic empowerment: 'Despite the large-scale engagement that UNHCR operations have with livelihoods programming, sustainable livelihood opportunities for women and adolescent girls of concern remain limited, specifically in terms of fully leveraging their transformative potential. Livelihood programmes are frequently based on restrictive assumptions linked to cultural gender norms. These assumptions about gender-appropriate livelihood activities limit women's possibilities for self-reliance. … In situations where governments do not give refugees the legal right to work, women are drawn to unregulated labour markets where they are at heightened risk of exploitation and abuse. … Additional challenges include the absence of childcare, limited access to education and training, and constraints on women's ability to own productive assets and control their own income. The lack of adequate economic opportunities heightens the risk of discrimination, SGBV, exploitation and abuse of women and girls, including sexual assault and harassment, forced and early girl child marriage, child labour and human trafficking' (UNHCR 2016: 8).

Sexual and gender-based violence (SGBV): 'Key challenges noted by operations include impunity for perpetrators of SGBV and the particular protection risks facing women and children living in urban areas. These include SGBV linked to detention, refoulement, exploitation and inadequate and/or overcrowded shelter. Both urban and camp settings

> suffer a shortage of safe shelters, weak and overburdened identification and referral systems, and a shortage of UNHCR staff and partners with SGBV expertise. Another challenge is the conflation of SGBV and gender equality – where SGBV work is understood as the sum total of all gender equality programming. This confusion contributes to an agency-wide lack of engagement with broader gender equality concerns' (UNHCR 2016: 9).

This report led to a further range of recommendations for realizing the five commitments and fed into making the gendered characteristics of forced migration a central focus in the development of the *Global Compact on Refugees*. Thus, for example, the UNHCR 2017 report *Achieving Gender Equality and Addressing Sexual and Gender-Based Violence in the Global Compact on Refugees* began by highlighting the following key point:

> Women and girls comprise at least 50 per cent of the refugee population, yet they are most often portrayed in policy and practice as a vulnerable minority. Their capacity to contribute to solutions often goes unrecognised and gender equality is an elusive goal. Despite the comprehensive law and policy developed over the past 30 years to address the protection needs of refugee women and girls, it is acknowledged that they still suffer endemic rape and gender-based violence (SGBV) which is both an outcome of and a major barrier to gender equality. This prevents access to many critical protection measures such as services, information, decent work, health and education, which are the basic requirements for self-reliance, and to durable solutions which should be equally available to both men and women. The immense social and economic capital and capacities of refugee women and girls are often underutilised, and their voices are silenced. Major barriers block their access to parity with men and boys. While

> this continues to occur, women and girls remain at risk and their potential involvement in problem solving is lost. (UNHCR 2017: 1)

The effects of this report are present throughout the *Global Compact on Refugees* and are particularly reflected in sections 74 and 75:

> 74. Women and girls may experience particular gender-related barriers that call for an adaptation of responses in the context of large refugee situations. In line with relevant international instruments and national arrangements, States and relevant stakeholders will seek to adopt and implement policies and programmes to empower women and girls in refugee and host communities, and to promote full enjoyment of their human rights, as well as equality of access to services and opportunities – while also taking into account the particular needs and situation of men and boys.
>
> 75. This will include contributions to promote the meaningful participation and leadership of women and girls, and to support the institutional capacity and participation of national and community-based women's organizations, as well as all relevant government ministries. Resources and expertise to strengthen access to justice and the security and safety of women and girls, including to prevent and respond to all forms of violence, including sexual exploitation and abuse, sexual- and gender-based violence and harmful practices, are called for; as is support to facilitate access to age-, disability- and gender-responsive social and health care services, including through recruitment and deployment of female health workers. Measures to strengthen the agency of women and girls, to promote women's economic empowerment and to support access by women and girls

> to education (including secondary and tertiary education) will be fostered. (UNHCR 2018a: 28–9)

The forced migration–gender nexus is thus well-recognized in the domain of international refugee policy. But are the women better protected? What points should we draw from this brief overview? The first is that there has been a significant learning process on the part of UNHCR with respect to the gendered character of forced migration, one in which some consultation with refugees has become a reasonably well-established practice since its age, gender and diversity approach was introduced in 2004. The second is that a range of very significant challenges remain in place for reasons relating to internal features of UNHCR (including its hierarchical bureaucratic structure), to issues of funding (and, relatedly, capacity), and to structural features of the refugee contexts (including local gender norms). The third is that legal recognition as a 'refugee' matters in terms of the applicability of these commitments, however partially they may be realized in practice. The fourth is that SGBV is a central issue in the gendered character of forced migration and consequently so too is SRH and effective access to SRH rights. This is stressed in some of the recommendations of the *Achieving Gender Equality* report:

> That SGBV risk identification and responses will be provided in cooperation with local services and national government ministries. These will include the early implementation of SGBV and health guidelines, paying attention to the additional risks faced by women and girls, and include access to safe shelters for women and children, the provision of sanitary materials, gender segregated, hygienic toilet and washing facilities within reception facilities. Effective and innovative prevention strategies will be developed in partnership with refugee communities. (UNHCR 2017: 4)

> That access is facilitated to refugee-sensitive national health, sexual and reproductive, and mental health services that address the specific health needs of women and girls, SGBV, the LGBTI *community* and other torture survivors and those with HIV/AIDS. (UNHCR 2017: 5)

This is not to say that other issues such as immediate security from SGBV in contexts of transit and settlement, and access to regular employment as a defence against livelihood contexts that exacerbate the risk of SGBV are not important. The same report is clear on this point in identifying and recommending support for ongoing needs:

> That on-going needs including comprehensive sexual and reproductive health, education, trauma counselling, adequate and safe shelter, information on legal options and access to justice, access to information, equal access to cash-based interventions, sustainable and appropriate livelihood opportunities, formal and non-formal education, recognition or fast-tracked conversion of educational and professional qualifications and the right to work will be provided as soon as is possible and in co-operation with host communities. (UNHCR 2017: 5)

Rather it is to point out that health, and in particular SRH, is an immediate and key interest for displaced women, and hence an important lens through which to address the availability of living minimally dignified lives to women and girls who are forcibly displaced. While UNHCR's recommendations have been central for the inclusion of gender-sensitive guidelines in relevant frameworks such as the *Global Compact on Refugees*, it begs the questions of whether these developments were able to translate into mechanisms of mainstreaming policy at the national level. Otherwise, the risk is that those guidelines remain nominal. It is at this stage, therefore, that we turn to track recognition of the intersection of gender, health and migration in policy.

Gender, migration and the human right to health: ambiguities in governance and responsibility

Global awareness around the feminization of migration, forced or otherwise, led to a gender perspective progressively becoming part of international and national normative instruments, alongside calls to respect international human rights commitments that are already in place.

All migrants enjoy, in principle, the protection of a complex set of international laws and treaties stemming from the 1948 Universal Declaration of Human Rights set forth rights and freedoms for, and the duty of protection to, all human beings. Since the Constitution of the World Health Organization (WHO) in 1946 and the Universal Declaration of Human Rights (UDHR) in 1948 the enjoyment of the highest attainable standard of health is put forward as a fundamental right of every human being without distinction of race, religion, political belief, economic or social condition (WHO 2003). In 2000, the UN Committee on Economic, Social and Cultural Rights (CESCR) issued 'General Comment 14',[3] a legally binding interpretation of the human right to health that codifies the right to health as 'the right to the enjoyment of the highest attainable standard of physical and mental health'. General Comment 14 acknowledges that the right to health is dependent on, and contributes to, the realization of other human rights, such as the rights to food, to an adequate standard of living, privacy and access to information. General Comment 14 also states freedoms and entitlements related to the right to health. Freedoms include the right to be free from non-consensual medical treatment, torture and other cruel, inhuman or degrading treatment or punishment, and the right to control one's body, including sexual and reproductive freedom. Entitlements, on its part, include the right to a system of health protection; the right to prevention, treatment and control of diseases; the right to healthy natural and workplace environments; and the right to health facilities, goods and services. Another important aspect in General Comment 14 is the importance of cultural sensitivity, or cultural appropriate medical provision, and the enjoyment of the highest attainable standard of health conducive to living a life in dignity.

What does this mean for displaced women and girls in transit or in temporary settlement, settling in new countries after forcibly fleeing conditions that threatened their rights and dignity, particularly their right to health?

According to Article 12 of the International Covenant on Economic, Social and Cultural Rights (ICESCR) states have a legal obligation 'to respect the right to health by, inter alia, refraining from denying or limiting access for all persons, including … asylum seekers and illegal immigrants, to preventive, curative and palliative health services … and abstaining from imposing discriminatory practices'.[4] In other words, restricting access to healthcare to populations because of their legal status is a violation of international human rights norms. This includes the recognition and integration of the SRH of migrants, which was accepted in the 1995 *Fourth World Conference on Women* in Beijing. Its Platform for Action stressed the importance of the human rights of women and girls, and their participation in society on equal terms, noting governmental obligations to:

> Ensure the full realization of the human rights of all women migrants, including women migrant workers, and their protection against violence and exploitation; introduce measures for the empowerment of documented women migrants, including women migrant workers; facilitate the productive employment of documented migrant women through greater recognition of their skills, foreign education and credentials, and facilitate

> their full integration into the labour force. (Beijing Declaration and Platform for Action 1995: 10, 58:k)

Likewise the Committee on the Elimination of Discrimination Against Women (CEDAW), General Comment 24, Article 12 on 'Women and Health' (1999) argued 'special attention should be given to the health needs and rights of women belonging to vulnerable and disadvantaged groups, such as migrant women, refugee and internally displaced women'. Its General Recommendation No. 26 on women migrant workers, provides specific guidance on essential sexual and reproductive health services that must be guaranteed by states (CEDAW 1999).

More recently, the Sustainable Development Goals (SDGs) recognized relevant specific goals to support its aim to 'leave no one behind' including SDG1 to reduce poverty, SDG3 to achieve universal health and wellbeing, and to ensure universal access to sexual and reproductive healthcare services, including services for family planning, information and education, and the integration of reproductive health services into national strategies and programmes (3.7); SDG 5 on gender equality, SDG 10 on reducing inequalities; SDG 11 on sustainable communities (particularly 11.5 on protection of displaced); and SDG 17 on partnership for development.

While the UN SDG principle of 'leave no one behind' is inclusive of migrants and refugees, the realization of universal healthcare for women and girls migrants requires better redressing of the conditions surrounding migration that often fuel health inequities and expose migrants to increased health inequalities. These include restrictive migration policies that may cause migrants to travel in a clandestine and risky manner using irregular means of transportation as well as anti-migrant sentiments that give them limited access to healthcare, education, and safe and dignified working and living conditions.

Some of this was picked up in the *Global Compact for Safe, Orderly and Regular Migration*, and the *Global Compact on*

Refugees, adopted in 2018 under the auspices of the United Nations, in its commitment to providing 'a gender-sensitive approach' where a guiding principle sets out a map for collective action to reverse conditions that create gender inequalities in terms of harms and barriers to the access of protection and healthcare by migrant women.

These frameworks make abundantly clear that health *rights*, including sexual and reproductive health rights, mean more than just *health* understood as a medical minimum. Ensuring that migrant women and girls are able to exercise full and equal freedoms and entitlements in relation to the right to health means upholding their place in society. For this to be achieved, delivering sexual and reproductive rights is a key part of the obligation of states, but so too is challenging conservative social norms in relation to how migrant women are treated and positioned in society, their social role, the place of migrant women in the workplace, and the family, are also central to the fulfilment of the right to health. But, as Hennebry and Petrozziello (2019) argue, despite their commitments, states are failing, deliberately or not, to convert international commitments into concrete sustained mechanisms for effective and sustainable measures that can redress systemic and structural gender inequalities.

Regional frameworks have been important means to put migrants' rights on the national agenda across Latin America. Yet, despite the rhetoric, these policies have not been fully implemented on the ground, and the safeguarding of the rights of migrants has profound limitations. As will be explored in Chapter 3, despite endorsing the relevant international instruments, Latin American countries have struggled to improve their national policies to protect migrants, particularly displaced women and girls, and even more dramatically, to develop a gender-responsive approach to migration and cooperation for migration and border governance. The regional governance infrastructure is complex, including organizations such as the Caribbean Community (CARICOM), the

Union of South American Nations (UNASUR), the Andean Community (CAN), the Southern Common Market (Mercosur) and the Pacific Alliance. Yet regional normative frameworks are often too weak or institutionally anaemic to level the playing field between migrants and nationals (Hujo and Piper 2015). For this reason, migration governance has been implemented unevenly and seemingly arbitrarily across the region, privileging 'migration management' approaches linked to security and employment regulations and labour rights (Acosta and Geddes 2014; Ceriani Cernadas 2018), rather than a rights-based approach to gender-responsive migration governance. Regional migration governance has failed in allocating responsibility and forms of protection as a shared responsibility for women and girls on the move. For this reason, with regard to gender, regional and national frameworks failed both to address harmful gender roles, norms, and relations as drivers of migration, as well as to guarantee gender-responsive services for women and girls in displacement and in places of abode. There is a clear gap between what governance systems can do in terms of promoting human rights, and how policy is actually translated into national laws and practice, particularly in relation to mainstreaming gender considerations into those laws and practices (Riggirozzi and Ryan 2022).

Zooming in to look at national responses, there are projects and programmes that aim at protecting migrant women and girls from harm and exploitation, but this is not enough to reverse the conditions that allow those harms and exploitation to occur in the first place. The everyday experience of women and girls in displacement suggest that social and cultural barriers to integration, acculturation stress, exclusion, violence and discrimination, changes in lifestyle and loss of family and friendship networks, and precarity and poverty are additional factors impacting the health of displaced women and girls (Starrs et al 2018; PAHO 2019a). Lack of training or understanding by staff at health facilities regarding the rights of migrants to receive care, cultural insensitivity, and embedded racism serve to generate discriminatory biases (Medecins Sans Frontieres 2017). Lack of access to disaggregated data in policy design and implementation, and lack of visibility, in many cases due to irregular migratory status, also obstruct displaced women and girls' access to protection, healthcare and rights more broadly. The COVID-19 pandemic accentuated pre-existing gender inequalities and exacerbated differential impacts on vulnerable populations, particularly displaced women, girls and the LGBTQI+ community, who have faced challenges related to forced evictions, lack of financial support or access to public funds, limited opportunities to earn a living, increasing chances of homelessness and destitution, gender-based violence, risks of exploitation and an increase in 'irregular' status among many who, because of restrictive policies and border closures, had no option but to enter countries via alternative crossings, overall extending and deepening situations of crisis that gave rise to migration and displacement in the first place (also Walsham 2022).

Nearly three decades have passed since the pioneering International Conference on Population and Development held in Cairo in 1994 and four since the adoption of CEDAW which confirmed sexual and reproductive health as a fundamental human right, and a necessary component for the wellbeing and inclusion of women and girls in society, including female migrants. Yet, more needs to be done at international, regional and national levels to redress gendered health inequalities – particularly those during and because of displacement.

The safeguarding of displaced women and girls' rights and reproductive health and rights in particular continues to be a cornerstone of the relentless fight for gender equality and for making effective the obligation on the part of states to respect, protect and ensure fulfilment of women and girls' sexual and reproductive rights. This is central to the analysis developed in this book.

Feminization of migration, displacement and health

Migration can act both as an enabler of opportunities and a constraint on freedoms and rights. Scholars have stressed that feminization is a core dimension of contemporary international migration; a trend that is not new to an increased globalized world and its externalities. In fact, as Donato and Gabaccia (2015) explore, women have always migrated, and often in substantial numbers. What is new is the trend – and in this respect the discussion about the feminization of migration is not so much about numbers, though these are significant, but rather the actual reasons for migration, including women increasingly migrating as the main economic providers, or 'breadwinners' for their households. In 2006, a report from the United Nations associated the feminization of migration with specific forms of migration produced by international commercialization of the migration of domestic workers and caregivers, the migration and trafficking of women for the sex industry, and the organized migration of women for marriage. This bleak situation increased attention on the gendered makeup of migrants and the risks that women on the move face, particularly in relation to sexual abuse, violence, trafficking and the exploitation of immigrant domestic workers.

Feminist work in forced migration studies underscored many of these issues highlighting situations where early marriage, female genital mutilation, gendered social stigma, gender-based violence and poverty force women and girls to flee (Freedman 2016, 2017; Menjívar and Walsh 2017; Patrinioti et al 2021). Migration scholars such as Aleinikoff and Zamore (2019) identified as 'necessary fleers' those forcibly displaced people who flee situations for reasons of practical necessity. For many women and girls in Latin America, and beyond, these reasons of practical necessity are gendered; conditions in their home country are intolerable and leave them as women with no reasonable alternative other than to flee the country because of direct threat or the prospects of physical insecurity or the loss of shelter and livelihood, or because their ability to care for themselves and their families are radically undermined.

Yet the pathways and border crossings many women and girls travel through are dangerous and expose them to gender violence, challenges and abuses which are liable to affect their sexual and reproductive health. Female forced migrants are particularly exposed to risks of exploitation, sexual violence and risky sexual behaviour for (economic) survival leading to increasing numbers of unwanted pregnancies, HIV and STIs, maternal death, and generalized precarity (UNFPA 2009, Ward and Marsh 2006; Madise and Onyango 2017; PAHO 2019a). For instance, Medecins Sans Frontieres (2020) reported that at Mexico's southern border, where migrants from Central America travelled on foot to avoid border controls, police and gangs, often in collaboration with one another, were reported as perpetrators of sexual and gendered violations (also Angulo-Pasel 2018). Particularly in the case of displaced people from Venezuela, many women reported other migrants or smugglers as perpetrators of sexual violence and other violations to their integrity and rights.

In addition to precarious and dangerous journeys, many women and girls suffer inadequate access to food and water, and experience traumatic situations during and because of the modalities and duration of travel. As Frida, an adolescent girl who migrated from Venezuela to Brazil, with her mother, walking for two days, claimed, "you just have to put your mind blank and continue on the path" (Manaus, 15 July 2021).

As migrants, and as women, many make daring decisions that may risk their own lives, but they do so for reasons of hope, a sense of responsibility and care, as well as an intrinsic drive for survival. Many are mothers caring for others who travel with them, or mothers that leave children behind, or in care of elderly relatives. The actual role in caregiving and responsibility are also gendered causes of forced migration. In difficult situations, many women make sacrifices for their children in, during and through migration. Fears for the safety of their children, especially girls, due to the threats of sexual abuses, are a constant for many female migrants during and after displacement, especially among those who travel alone or are single mothers.

Once in the migratory journey, many choices that women and girls (are forced to) make to respond to, and cope with, risks faced during displacement may themselves bring about new risks to their health, wellbeing and dignity more broadly. This is what Garbett et al (forthcoming) identified as 'the paradox of choice'. Women and girls are forced to make decisions that compromise their wellbeing, autonomy and dignity, and yet that seems to be a choice of necessity as it enables continuing the journey. For instance, women may (or feel forced to) exchange sex for food, protection or transport to continue the passing or crossing, or for subsistence in places of abode. One migrant woman interviewed in Bogotá, Colombia, recalled:

> 'Many people take the easy way out, which is prostitution … selling their bodies, things that they did not do back in Venezuela … because perhaps they have necessities, they have to feed their children.' (Nancy, Bogotá, 19 August 2021)

Likewise, many are subject to changing demands and abuse by smugglers in the course of the journey. One 25-year-old interviewee described,

> 'We travelled by *trocha*,[5] with my husband. … We had a bad experience at the end of the whole route of the *trocha*, because some rogues subjected us … they wanted us to pay more, but we paid before … but they wanted me to pay … [and demanded] that I slept with them, and so, well, that was a bad experience.' (Flavia, Manaus, 7 May 2021)

The accepted reality that migrant women and girls are likely to suffer sexual abuse and rape during the migratory journey – the almost normalized situation of gendered sexual violence – leads many women and adolescents to use long-acting contraception before travelling; this is the main preventative method in preparation of fleeing and in regard to sexual and reproductive health (Vazquez-Quesada et al 2021). Between 60 and 80 per cent of female migrants travelling through Mexico are raped along the way, according to estimates from a study by Amnesty International (Amnesty International 2010; also Soria-Escalante et al 2021: 28). The risk increases according to age, particularly for girls and adolescents who travel alone or accompanied by a smuggler who leads the way to the border of the country of destination. Girls and adolescents travelling alone can also easily become targets of human trafficking networks for the purpose of sexual exploitation.

Gender-specific challenges that women and girls face in displacement are often concealed and unreported. Situations of harm and vulnerability not only affect the autonomy and wellbeing of women and girls in displacement but also their opportunities for just integration in societies of abode. Many migrants experience gendered health vulnerabilities as a consequence of sex exploitation or exploitation in the labour market in the form of informal, precarious and unpaid/underpaid care work (Delgado Wise et al 2013, Bastia and Piper 2019). These factors, coupled with denial of protection and access to health services during the migratory journey, or after arrival for legal reasons relating to migrant status, discriminatory practices and anti-migrant sentiments, are all determinants of health status, of opportunities for access to healthcare services as well as of healthcare seeking behaviour (Starrs et al 2018; Wickramage and Annunziata 2018). As Sheylimar claimed in an interview, "migration represents being judged" (Manaus, 17 July 2021).

Many feminist scholars have called attention to how social and institutional contexts, in transit and in places of abode, reproduce gendered health inequalities and injustices (Piper 2009; Herrera 2013; Freedman 2016, 2017). For example, (lack of) legal status, the policies which grant or deny access to migrant-friendly health and social services, and the working and living conditions of migrants are determinants of accessibility to healthcare and health status (see also Fleischman et al 2015; Ho et al 2019). We develop this point further in Chapter 3. Meanwhile we build on these concerns to argue that there is a migration–gender–health nexus defined by gendered risks and vulnerabilities that affect displaced women and girls' health, particularly their sexual and reproductive health, during and because of the migration process. It is in this key that we draw out critical implications for how protection is and should be conceived and how regulations, policies and services in places of transit and abode should address the circumstances in which 'necessary fleers' find themselves as well as for secure conditions that enable displaced women and girls 'to rebuild their social lives in relation to their immediate environment and to engage in autonomous choices with respect to their future' (Owen 2018: 31).

Protection systems, and health systems in particular, in host communities have responsibilities, legally and morally, to support women and girls in displacement. Of course, accommodating the sudden arrival of newcomers presents a challenge for host governments and, in the case of developing countries, there is further pressure on communities already suffering the consequences of unequal development and poverty. Here their ability to deliver basic (health) services and infrastructure can be hugely compromised (Rivillas et al 2018; Angulo-Pasel 2018; Abubakar et al 2018). As a consequence, it is often international organizations and non-state actors (including charities and religious institutions) who try to fill the gap of attention to the health needs of the displaced and supporting – often in ad hoc ways – their human right to health.

Building on this, we claim that generating gender equity and fulfilment of rights of displaced women and girls should bring into focus national actors, such as state agencies' and health systems, as well as regional and multilateral international actors' obligations in ways that protect the right to health of displaced women and girls, redressing the conditions that affect their prospects of wellbeing and address health inequalities, enabling all migrant women and girls to rebuild their lives with dignity, regardless of their migrant status, as will be further explored throughout the book.

Feminization and gendered causes of Venezuelan forcibly displacement

Migration in Latin America is not new but the magnitude of intraregional migration in Central and South America has been an unprecedented occurrence in the past five years. Since the first so-called 'caravan' of over 7,000 spontaneously self-organized people trekking from Honduras, El Salvador and Guatemala to march through Mexico towards the US in 2018 to the nearly 7 million who fled Venezuela since 2016, it became apparent that the lack of protection from their governments, poverty and precarious living conditions drive thousands of women and girls to leave their homes.

While Central America has a history of mass migration, heightened by recent history of gang violence, South America was taken by surprise by the rapid and large scale displacements from Venezuela since 2014. Venezuela has seen a fast turnaround of events that has resulted in the most complex humanitarian crisis in Venezuelan and South American history. From being home to the world's largest oil reserves, Venezuela turned into South America's poorest economy, with an annual hyperinflation surreally close to 500,000 per cent since 2018 and poverty levels affecting approximately 90 per cent of the population (World Bank 2021: 14). This is a striking contrast to previous decades when Venezuela was a focal point in the continental promise of a more direct and inclusive alternative to dominant marketized approaches to development and democracy. In fact, at the end of the 1990s, governments across South America began embarking on various 'post-neoliberal' experiments which for more than a decade seemed to work, and where Venezuela was a central financial and ideological driver. In Venezuela, social, political and economic reforms between 1998 and 2012 helped cut poverty by a spectacular 50 per cent, and extreme poverty by 65 per cent. Venezuela also became an important referent and a pioneer in transnational social policies, funding health policies across the region. For example, under a flagship programme called Oil for Doctors, Venezuela subsidized oil exports to Cuba in exchange for deployments of Cuban medics and medical training programmes (Webb-Vidal and Frank 2004), expanding the number of primary care physicians in the public sector and supporting the Barrio Adentro programme that provided free basic medical care in Venezuela (Muntaner et al 2006). Likewise, through Mission Miracle, Venezuela provided free eye care to people across the region, while other Venezuelan initiatives tackled the needs of people with disabilities across Central and South America (see Riggirozzi 2012).

But these remarkable projects all depended on revenue from Venezuela's oil bonanza and accumulated reserves. Once the country was hit by an international oil industry downturn, the result was a string of shortages and widespread social deprivation – and a spiralling socio-political crisis. Along with the economic collapse, politically the country saw rapidly expanding authoritarianism following the death of President Hugo Chavez in 2013 and the takeover by Nicolás Maduro. The humanitarian, economic and political crises in Venezuela have since worsened and been coupled with international sanctions. Caritas (2017) reported a dramatic reduction in food imports and the high cost of food led to food deprivation and hunger, including situations of child malnutrition in parts of Venezuela. Moreover, a deterioration of public finances impacted the provision of health services, leading to a significant increase in cases of measles and diphtheria, previously eradicated diseases, as well as tuberculosis and malaria. This critical situation was compounded by the lack of essential medicines – in the region of 85 per cent – and a collapsing hospital infrastructure, including lack of electricity and water as well as supplies such as gloves and syringes (Van Praag 2019).

While these intersecting crises affect the population in general, they have a disproportionate effect on women and girls. For example, food shortages have a particularly adverse effect on female caregivers and heads of households, who are often responsible for feeding children and caring for the elderly. Reports show that women spend up to ten hours a day searching for food, in some cases exchanging sex for food. According to the OHCHR (2018), there were high rates of malnutrition among pregnant women in poor neighbourhoods, and a significant increase of infant and maternal mortality rates.

In addition, the sharp decline in medical infrastructure impacted women of childbearing age as they particularly struggled to access contraceptive methods. Even before the humanitarian crisis, Venezuela had one of the highest teenage pregnancy rates in the world (Cawthorne 2014). To tackle that problem, the socialist government rolled out entitlements to contraception in 2005 but since then the country's stocks of contraceptives have fallen by 90 per cent (Albaladejo 2018). The contraception shortage, coupled with the decline in medical infrastructure, fuelled a rise in sexually transmitted diseases, particularly HIV, increased maternal mortality rates, the risk of unwanted pregnancy (a widely recognized problem for adolescent girls) and consequently unsafe abortions (United Nations High Commissioner for Human Rights 2019: 18). More and more women and girls are seeking out illegal abortions and even sterilizations (Marillier and Squires 2018). Deteriorations of hospitals and maternity clinics also led to limited pre- and post-natal care. Amnesty International (2018) reported that between 2015 and 2016 maternal deaths increased by 65 per cent and infant mortality by 30 per cent, moving backwards to the prevailing situation 25 years ago in Venezuela. Not only has Venezuela the highest maternal mortality rates in the region (125 deaths per 100,000 live births) but also 13 per cent of those are due to unsafe abortions (see Van Praag 2019; Luigi-Bravo and Gill 2022).

As we explore in more detail in Chapter 4, it is not surprising in this context that health and SRH in particular became reasons why many women found it necessary to flee in the hope of living a life in health, with dignity and free from harm, fear and gender-based violence.

Understanding the Venezuelan migration crisis from a gender perspective is about conceptualizing and making visible stories and struggles of human rights of women and girls that were forced to leave their place of residence, but also turning attention to policy agendas at the international, regional and national levels responsible for managing and delivering health needs in migration and beyond.

Conclusion

Good health for women and girls on the move and a safeguard of human rights for all are central to any durable solution to challenges of mass and forced displacement. Yet health, and sexual and reproductive health in particular, is one of the bleakest sites of harmful experiences that affect displaced women and girls' rights, freedoms, dignity and opportunities to integrate in society.

This has been highlighted by international agendas based on recognition of the link between health and poverty. Gender equality, the empowerment of women and girls, and healthy lives and wellbeing with the transformative promise *of leaving no one behind* are constitutive elements of the SDGs in accordance with the Programme of Action of the International Conference on Population and Development and the Beijing Platform for Action and the outcome documents of their review conferences. Momentum followed with the *Global Compact for Migration* in 2018 and the establishment of the United Nations Network on Migration. Yet there remain very major gaps in adequately integrating a gender perspective for the provision of SRH and important rights protections in international and regional governance (Hennebry and Petrozziello 2019).

Two immediate consequences arise from this, and that will be the subject of analysis in subsequent chapters. First, the health of female migrants, and SRH in particular, lags behind the promise of principles of protection; there are protection gaps in which international and national laws, norms, material circumstances and actors in specific contexts should perform the duty of ensuring protection of forcibly displaced but are not successful in doing so. Second, millions of women and girls in Latin America are caught in the vicious spiral of vulnerability to endemic violence and humanitarian crisis that takes specific gendered forms of violence and forced displacement (with its own risks for women's health, and sexual and reproductive health in particular). But their access to protective and enabling public services that can secure health rights during the journey and in places of abode is typically confronted by barriers that compromise the responsibility and responses that states assume internationally as much as the delivery of responsive protection and services in places of temporary or permanent settlement. Throughout the book, we argue that although international commitments to non-nationals are normally organized in a distinctive way, one that creates different sets of protection frameworks for migrants and refugees, forcibly displaced women as necessary fleers are entitled to protection and basic (human) rights for reasons beyond their assigned categories. Chapter 2 will particularly take a look at how this migrant–refugee distinction affects governance of female displacement and women's unequal access to rights, and defend the use of a different framework, which goes beyond this binary governance, protecting women for reasons of practical necessity. We develop these claims further in the coming chapters as we problematize the meaning of flight for Venezuelan women and girls, and ask whether existing normative frameworks not only address the challenges of SRH needs and rights but also structure practices in accordance with those needs and the responsibilities of states in meeting national and international goals.

TWO

Problematizing the Migrant–Refugee Distinction in Latin America

The general concept 'migrant' encompasses a heterogeneous range of individuals who move from one place to another for different reasons. Migrants may move within or across state borders. Migration may involve pendular, circular, or return movements; transit, settlement, or just travel for short periods of time. What forms a specific migration may change depending on the situation, the dynamics of movement, and on the migrants' opportunities to exercise choice, desire, and agency. As a legal concept and in policy contexts, however, 'migrant' is distinguished from, on the one hand, 'visitors' (such as tourists) and, on the other hand, 'refugees' (and related categories). Our focus in this chapter is on the distinction between 'migrants' and 'refugees', and the implications of the ways this distinction is mobilized in, and plays out across, legal, political and social contexts with significant effects on the rights and wellbeing of those subject to this schema. As noted in the last chapter, this is particularly important in the case of displaced Venezuelans, especially Venezuelan women and girls. The primary reasons for their displacement are extreme poverty, lack of medical services, gender-based violence, and lack of sustenance and hence they are not straightforwardly encompassed by categories of international refugee protection and, therefore, may fail to be recognized as entitled to the necessary protection and assistance, becoming vulnerable to yet more rights violations, even in their already very fragile circumstances.

We begin by considering debates around the category of 'refugee' and the political role of such debates within the current international refugee regime, before turning to the way in which the refugee/migrant distinction establishes a rights hierarchy in the reception and treatment of border-crossing people. Against this backdrop, we argue for a framework in which the categories of displaced persons to whom international assistance and protection need to be provided is specified by the concept of 'necessary fleers' (Aleinikoff and Zamore 2019) which denotes all those for whom conditions in their home state make flight across a border a reasonable and justifiable recourse for securing basic human rights. These are people who may reasonably conclude that they have no alternative other than to leave the country and enter a migration process because of a direct threat or the prospects of physical insecurity or the loss of shelter and livelihood, or because their ability to care for themselves and their families are radically undermined. It is in this key that we identify necessary fleers from Venezuela in order to draw out the critical implications for how protection is conceived and how regulations, policies and services in places of transit and abode address the circumstances in which these 'necessary fleers' find themselves and how they enable them 'to rebuild their social lives in relation to their immediate environment and to engage in autonomous choices with respect to their future' (Owen 2018: 31).

Framing the forcibly displaced as *necessary fleers* allows us to contest the sociological assumptions and normative categories that underpin current asylum/migration governance, and which are responsible for leaving many migrants in vulnerable situations and without the international protection that they need and which their claim to dignity requires. The concept of *necessary fleers* also supports the argument of this book, which claims that a robust ethics of the forcibly displaced in Latin America must be articulated, going beyond the current refugee system, to encompass the specific nature and complexities of displacements in the Americas. The urgency of this task is driven not least by the recognition that current practices of asylum are insufficient to provide protection to many displaced Venezuelan women and girls migrating to or transiting through Brazil and Colombia, and that protection gaps create further vulnerabilities that affect in particular their health needs and rights, all of which as we explore in Chapter 4.

The politics of refuge

There is both a sociological and a normative dimension to debates surrounding the figure of the refugee, and these are necessarily linked. To draw this point out, we will briefly review the emergence and development of the international refugee regime, before turning to critical discussion of the debates addressing this system of protection.

According to the United Nations Convention Relating to the Status of Refugees of 1951,[1] a refugee is:

> One who owing to a well-founded fear of being persecuted for reasons of race, religion, nationality [as belonging to a 'people'], membership of a social group or political opinion is outside the country of his nationality [as membership of a state] and is unable or, owing to such fear, is unwilling to avail himself of the protection of that country; or who, not having a nationality and being outside the country of his habitual residence … is unable, or, owing to such fear, is unwilling to return to it.[2]

All those who flee their home countries for the reasons stated in this treaty are (in principle) entitled to the right to enjoy international protection and have the status of refugees. However, the specification of the category of refugees identified here is narrow, responsive to a set of specific European post-Second World War concerns and originally subject to geographic and temporal limits that reflected this fact (until these were abolished by the 1967 Protocol). Such limited scope has given rise to critical analysis of the Refugee Convention as representing a 'distinctly colonial' and 'exclusionary agenda' (Krause 2021).

The removal of geographic and temporal barriers to the 1951 Convention has though only focused attention on the narrow construal of the criteria of refugeehood and their relation to Europe's mid-20th century experience of forced displacement in the emerging Cold War context. Awareness that the legal specification of refugees in the 1951 Convention had been developed for the post-war context in Europe and did not fit well with the pragmatics of forced migration in the developing world led the Organisation of African Unity (OAU) to develop a regional refugee convention – the 1969 OAU *Convention Governing the Specific Aspects of Refugee Problems in Africa* – that was rooted in acknowledgement of the newly universalized 1951 Convention but extended the scope of refugeehood to cover those fleeing the breakdown of public order and generalized violence in response to the postcolonial African context. Such regional developments were continued in the 1984 *Cartagena Declaration* following the expansive path set by the OAU to cover Latin America and, most recently, the attempt by the EU to develop a more restrictive but legally binding *Common European Asylum System*. At the same time, the growth of the international human rights regime – especially since the 1970s – has supported important interpretive developments including increasing acknowledgement of claims that this definition should be read to encompass persecution by non-state actors from which the state is not disposed to protect citizens and that threats or conduct amounting to persecution can take gender-specific (and other social identity-specific) forms as well as of appeals to the category 'membership of a social group' (encompassing, for example, LGBTIQ+ persons).[3] These judicial developments have widened the practical scope of the Convention, but perhaps the most significant development of the interaction of human rights law and the international refugee regime though has been the expanded principle of *non-refoulement* in which the norm of non-refoulement established in the Convention is extended to cover persons who do not fall under the Convention criteria of refugeehood but have human rights-based grounds not to be returned to their home state. Such 'complementary protection' is 'typically granted where the treatment feared does not reach the level of severity of "persecution," or where there is a risk of persecution, but it is not linked to one of the Refugee Convention grounds' (McAdam 2014: 204–5).

These developments can be seen as responses to the general normative problem confronted by the definition of refugeehood which is nicely expressed by Shacknove (1985: 275):

> An overly narrow conception of 'refugee' will contribute to the denial of international protection to countless people in dire circumstances whose claim to assistance is impeccable. Ironically, for many persons on the brink of disaster, refugee status is a privileged position. In contrast to other destitute people, the refugee is eligible for many forms of international assistance, including material relief, asylum, and permanent resettlement. Conversely, an overly inclusive conception is also morally suspect and will, in addition, financially exhaust relief programs and impune the credibility of the refugee's privileged position among host populations, whose support is crucial for the viability of international assistance programs.

However, while both the OAU Convention and the Cartagena Declaration can be seen as attempts to address this dilemma in regional contexts, and fundamentally from a Southern perspective, these attempts also point to the intersection of the sociological and normative dimensions of refugee protection. On the one hand, in adapting the criteria of refugeehood for their regional contexts, they prefigure a point stressed by Crawley and Skleparis (2018) that a categorization of 'migrant vs refugee' oversimplifies the experience of people in displacement and the complex relationship between political, social and economic drivers of migration. Moreover, the use of these categories risks not only unjust treatment of many who migrate, but also illustrates the problem of policy makers ignoring 'the complexities of migration in the construction of policy categories while taking full advantage of this complexity when it suits their political interests' (2018: 58). On the other hand, in simply expanding the range of criteria on the basis of which the status of refugehood can be claimed, they do not escape the general problem of privileging particular types of forced migration or grounds of flight over others in terms of entitlement to international protection.

The debate concerning 'who is a refugee' has three further dimensions that are politically significant for our concerns. The first arises from the fact that, despite the development of regional frameworks, the 1951 Convention remains the key international instrument of refugee protection with the consequence, as Behrman (2018: 45) notes that 'for most people forcibly displaced around the world, refugee law is at best an irrelevance and at worst a barrier to protection'. It is at best an irrelevance for most of those who flee because they are not covered by its provisions; it is at worst a barrier because a state may use it as a reason to bar entry and protection to those in flight who do not fall under its auspices. The second is that the Convention leaves it to the legal systems of states to interpret the definition of the refugee that it supplies. The international refugee regime did not provide a right to asylum for displaced individuals but only a right to *seek* asylum, and states were given the 'right' to interpret it, defining who is (or is not) a refugee. It is noteworthy that states have exercised the liberty of interpreting the Convention's concept themselves in ways that have aimed at increasingly constricting its scope to meet their political interests. As Ní Ghráinne (2020: 142, 341) notes 'states increasingly interpret the 1951 Convention to suit their interests of limiting their refugee intake'. The third is that the contrast between the narrow Convention definition and the wider policy use of the term 'refugee' by UNHCR has generated a general indeterminacy in public political discourse that oscillates between a (narrow) legal-political conception and a (wide) humanitarian conception that is open to political exploitation and is mobilized in, for example, rhetorical distinctions – such as that between 'genuine' and 'bogus' asylum seekers, or that between 'deserving' refugees and 'queue-jumpers' – in order to limit the expansion of the international refugee law frameworks, criminalize irregular migration pathways, and further restrict access to rights by forcibly displaced individuals who are either awaiting legal determination of their status (such as asylum seekers) or have not been recognized as refugees under a state's legal system.

The efforts by states to exploit the indeterminacy of the public discourse surrounding refugees in order to limit their protection responsibilities have not gone unchallenged. For example, in the 1990s, refugee rights advocates and displaced individuals themselves fought for the recognition of gender-based violence as a type of persecution which fell under the umbrella of the 1951 Convention concept of refugee. Today this is generally undisputed, especially after UNHCR's guidelines concerning the protection of refugee women (1991) and regarding gender-related persecution (2002), but this outcome is the result of processes of legal dispute and political struggle that continued at least until the end of the 1990s (Arbel et al 2014). Similarly, a UNHCR guideline referring to persecution related to sexuality and gender identity was only issued in 2012. All in all, the absence of 'sexuality and gender' as reasons for persecution under the 1951 Convention concept prevented many women and LGBTQ+ people from accessing the right to international protection as refugees for many decades (UNHCR 2013).

The expansion of the conception of refugeehood in the 1951 Convention in different regional contexts and the extension of the scope of the Convention's conception through judicially mediated political struggles is indeed able to account for the protection of some forced migrants that would otherwise not have been incorporated under the Convention's scope. However, as we have noted, such developments do not overcome the problem of adjusting to the dynamic nature of forced migration and are liable to leave many individuals outside the existing frameworks of protection. As feminist and LGBTQ+ groups fought for recognition of gender- and sexuality-based violence as grounds for refugeehood in the 1990s and 2000s that were eventually encompassed within a wider interpretation of the Refugee Convention, debates now involve climate displacement, survival refugees, and food refugees, among others. Consider for a moment the provisions of the Cartagena Declaration which states:

> the definition or concept of a refugee to be recommended for use in the region is one which, in addition to containing the elements of the 1951 Convention and the 1967 Protocol, includes among refugees persons who have fled their country because their lives, safety or freedom have been threatened by generalized violence, foreign aggression, internal conflicts, massive violation of human rights or other circumstances which have seriously disturbed public order.

Now reflect on the position of pregnant women confronted by the collapse of adequate maternity care in the Venezuelan health service. In 2019, Luisangela Correa, a surgeon at the Concepcion Palacios hospital (Caracas's main maternity hospital) highlighted that "the blood banks and medicine cabinets are empty, the power and water regularly cut out – and women and girls are dying needlessly". She noted that "infection rates at the maternity hospital are high because cleaners do not have disinfectants to wash away bacteria and there are no sterilizers for doctors to clean their equipment" before going on to say "Currently, maternity is a risk for Venezuelan women, as it is for babies … many give birth at home, in the street. … And there are no blood banks. Any complications from heavy bleeding is a very big risk of death for a patient" (see Moloney 2019). A year previously in 2018 a *Lancet* editorial had already noted:

> The last official report from the Venezuelan Ministry of Health was published in 2016 (*Boletin Epidemiologico*) and the then Health Minister, Antonieta Corporale, was rewarded by being sacked immediately thereafter by Nicolas Maduro, who has been leading the country since 2013 (Venezuela has had 17 different ministers of health in the past 20 years). The results of this report were highlighted in a *Lancet* World Report in August, 2017, which noted the untenable situation in Venezuela. This government report revealed a 65 per cent increase in maternal mortality and a 30 per cent increase in infant mortality, with 11,466 infants dying during 2016.

Under these conditions, it is unsurprising that, from 2016, pregnant Venezuelan women have chosen to cross borders:

> 'My baby would have died if I had stayed. There was no food or medicine, no doctors', said Maria Teresa Lopez as she fed her daughter Fabiola, who was born on Monday night by caesarean in the maternity hospital of Boa Vista, the capital of Brazil's Roraima border state. (Doce 2018)

She is not alone in reaching this judgement: 'Births of Venezuelan babies at the Boa Vista maternity hospital surged to 566 last year and 571 in the first half of 2018, from 288 in 2016 when the flow of Venezuelan refugees began, the Roraima health department said' (see Doce 2018).

Do the pregnant Venezuelan women who flee across the border to, for example, Colombia satisfy the criteria established by the Cartagena Declaration? Not obviously. Rather it would require some significant and creative interpretation of either the 'massive human rights violation' or the 'other circumstances which have seriously disturbed public order' clauses to make such a case. Do these women have compelling and justifiable reasons to take flight to another state where there is a functioning maternal health system? Without doubt.

The issue that we have identified here concerning the figure of the refugee as specified in terms of particular grounds of flight thus concerns the construction of a categorical distinction between refugees and migrants which assigns some forced migrants to the former category for whom the international community has clear obligations of protection and others to the latter category in which there is no such immediate responsibility. The problem of the refugee/migrant distinction is not that we have no reasons to distinguish between persons requiring international protection and persons for whom such protection is not required, but that the refugee/migrant distinction both does not track this distinction and its failure to track it enables a politics that is harmful to those wrongly denied international protection. The displacement of Venezuelan women is exemplary of this failure and highlights the need for novel gendered understandings of forced migration.

The migrant–refugee distinction and hierarchies of rights

Recall Shacknove's (1985) remark in highlighting the general normative problem confronted by the specification of refugeehood: 'Ironically, for many persons on the brink of disaster, refugee status is a privileged position.' This draws attention to the point that the legal distinction between refugees and migrants can have very significant implications for access to international protection; indeed, Hamlin (2021) argues it 'makes a clear distinction between those to whom an obligation is owed and those who are less deserving of an international response', while Awad and Natarajan (2018) remark that it 'arbitrarily creates hierarchies of suffering as means of legitimating international protection in certain areas and abdicating responsibility in others'. As a consequence, many of those who have fallen through the categorical cracks of refugeehood, despite being in need of protection, may be met with a less than humane treatment while in displacement. Thus, a key reason that the debates around the concept 'refugee' matter is that, for all the problems confronted by people seeking asylum and the obstacles that states construct to their being able to successfully claim refugee status, the figure of the refugee denotes an exceptional status in that states are obliged under the strict norm of non-refoulement not to return refugees to any other state in which they are at risk of persecution or other breaches of their human rights. As a result, the figure of the refugee is a legally privileged one since they represent an exception to the sovereignty rule that states have the right to control crossings in their borders. This, in turn, shapes how border crossers are treated (Hamlin 2021) – either under the exceptional or the sovereign rule. This is particularly salient to the tensions between abstract human rights and the lived experiences of human rights by migrants, as in practice, 'generous human rights principles have often been interpreted by courts in a way that effectively served to exclude many migrants from full protection' (Dembour and Kelly 2012: 3). Although all migrants should have access to human rights, in actual fact, issues of their enforcement, accountability and materialization almost always depend on their social-legal status.

If we consider the 1951 Refugee Convention, it is important to note that the Convention marks out the distinctiveness of the refugee not only in terms of a legitimate claim to the protection of a state which is not their own (legally expressed in the norm of non-refoulement) but also by positioning the figure of the refugee as a rights-bearing subject between citizen and resident non-citizens ascribing some rights to refugees on an equal basis to citizens and others on a basis at least as favourable as that of the most privileged resident non-citizens. The point of this provision covering employment, housing, welfare, education and health was to secure the social autonomy of refugees and enable their integration into the host society. The 1951 Convention also ascribes to the state of asylum the duty to ensure that the refugee enjoys the assistance necessary for international travel and protection when abroad that would normally be provided by the refugee's state of nationality. Against this legal backdrop, it is unsurprising that the figure of the refugee appears as one privileged relative to other forced migrants: in principle, they cannot be returned to danger and they enjoy a wide range of rights. And while this privilege may be most starkly revealed in juxtaposing Convention refugees with those whose reasons for flight are not encompassed by the Convention's focus on persecution on specific grounds, the problem that it reveals in which the refugee/migrant distinction serves to elide the ethical significance of some other forms of non-voluntary displacement has general application to regional as well as international refugee law.

Yet the migrant–refugee distinction does not merely construct a legal hierarchy of rights or access to international protection, it is also central to a range of political dynamics that shape the field of (lack of) protection of forced migrants.

The first of these arises in the context of a general and enduring feature of the international refugee regime, namely, that 'protection, assistance, and durable solutions are provided to refugees at levels that fall well below needs, and responsibility is allocated based on proximity' and 'despite the fact that this state of affairs has persisted for decades, no adequate institutional mechanisms – whether legal, political, or operational – have been created to ensure more equitable and predictable responsibility-sharing' (Betts et al 2017: 16). This is driven by the character of refugee protection as a global public good and is currently expressed as a situation in which 85 per cent of the world's refugees are hosted in states in developing regions of the world that are proximate to refugee-producing states because, given 'their usually porous borders and strong normative obligations to offer asylum', these states 'face very little alternative other than to open their borders to refugees'. However, 'those richer states further afield face only a discretionary duty to contribute through responsibility-sharing, assuming that their access barriers work, and they are able to prevent refugees from arriving spontaneously' (Betts et al 2017: 30). Hence, the latter have no incentive to engage in fair responsibility sharing. It is notable that as the scope of refugeehood has expanded, so too have the efforts of non-neighbouring states to create 'access barriers', to prevent the arrival at their territory of refugees through the use of non-entry practices (Fitzgerald 2019) and other measures designed to obstruct the safe passage of refugees. This political development has been enabled by the mobilization of the distinction between 'genuine' and 'bogus' refugees that is predicated on the prior distinction between refugees and migrants and the way it ignores the moral claims of forced migrants who do not fall under the specification of refugeehood. More recently, it has also been supported by the political construction of a distinction between 'proper' or 'deserving' refugees who patiently await an imagined resettlement[4] process (this despite the fact that there are only annual resettlement spaces for only about 1 per cent of refugees) and refugees who engage in 'secondary migration' (that is those who move on from the state for first refuge) and can then be treated as 'migrants' who are presented as abusing the refugee system. The refugee/migrant distinction thus serves an enabler of ideological measures aimed at limiting access to international protection to refugees as well as forced migrants in general.

This global context has given rise to a second problem, namely, protection of refugee rights in hosting states. As Aleinikoff and Owen (2022:11) argue:

> States and international organizations have been hesitant to insist that countries of asylum respect human rights commitments (or to condition aid on respect for such rights) for the simple reason that hosting states, if they feel undue pressure from countries elsewhere in the world, have the power to send refugees home and close their borders to new arrivals or to incentivize the onward movement of refugees. There has thus been an unholy grand bargain at the heart of the international refugee regime: states of the Global South take refugees in so long as states of the Global North provide (albeit inadequate) financial support and don't press human rights concerns. This is not to condemn hosting states. Most are trying to make the best of a bad situation: how to respect international obligations to leave their borders open to fleers from danger in a world where others neglect their responsibility to share the burden.

This is also not to say that the distinction between migrant and refugee does not matter in Global South contexts, only that the way that it matters is liable to vary across different states in terms of their specific histories and how they are situated in relation to large scale flows of forced migrants.

This, in turn, points to a third feature: in practice the apparently categorical distinction between migrants and refugees can give rise to a plurality of intermediate statuses – such as, for example, 'temporary protection' and 'humanitarian leave to remain' – that may represent both a reluctance to grant Convention refugee status and an acknowledgement that there are grounds for (some degree of) protection that do not fall under the scope of the Convention specification of refugeehood. This feature arguably supports, and is further complicated by, the choices of states concerning whether to use the legal framework of refugeehood to address significant displacement events, where the political construction of this choice as a legitimate response is particularly supported in contexts where the causes of displacement can be presented as falling outside the usual grounds of refugee claims.

All of these political dynamics are salient in the regional context of Latin America because intraregional forced migration in Latin America is typically large scale (for example, the cases of Haitians in Brazil and Chile, Colombians in Ecuador, and Venezuelans in Brazil, Peru and Colombia, among others) and may be for a mixed range of reasons (including environmental reasons, conflict, widespread violence, poverty, political persecution). The 1984 Cartagena Declaration was a milestone in the region as it recognized the need to widen the scope of refugeehood in order to increase these border crossers' chances of acquiring protection. Despite its conceptual and symbolic importance, however, it has seldom been applied in practice:

> The regional refugee definition in the Cartagena Declaration was meant to provide a concise reference point to expand protection while swiftly responding to the growing plight of refugees who did not fulfil the 1951 Convention definition. Almost thirty years later, the failure of many Latin American states to champion the regional refugee definition, to take concrete steps to make it operable and to faithfully apply its contents has implications that go far beyond the side lining of the regional refugee definition. Officials processing asylum claims do not appear to know how to apply the regional refugee definition in a consistent and coherent manner. This element remains an important regional challenge for the protection of refugees in Latin America. The issues that are at stake are the loss of solidarity toward persons fleeing generalized violence or conflict in the region and

> the overshadowing of the refugee protection regime by the growing focus on security. (Reed-Hurtado 2013: 32)

As most intraregional migration flows in Latin America have been characterized by 'structural factors' pertaining to 'different levels of economic and social development' (ECLAC 2000: 22), the Cartagena Declaration was a very welcome addition to the region's body of asylum laws. The choice by states not to apply it in practice highlights a first problem.

Thus, for example, in the case of those fleeing Venezuela, despite many Venezuelans' desire to settle in Colombia and yet despite the incorporation of the Cartagena Declaration into Colombian law, only circa 100 Venezuelans out of 10,000 asylum seekers have been recognized refugees, with around 1.7 million Venezuelan migrants in the country (UNHCR 2019).[5] This not only demonstrates the political choice not to apply the Cartagena provisions, it also highlights that normative consequences of this choice for those displaced persons. Since the start of the Venezuelan displacement, Colombia's approach has been to provide a temporary migration status to Venezuelans who arrived within a given time period but to leave those who arrived after this time with an irregular status. By 2021, according to the IOM (2021), an astonishing proportion of Venezuelan children in Colombia had an irregular status, with only 15 per cent of them having documents establishing a regular migrant status. Most of them crossed the border irregularly and lived on the streets, lacking basic rights. In fact, less than 50 per cent of the surveyed children had access to education, and the main reason given for absence of schooling was the lack of official documents. Colombia's ad hoc migration management of Venezuelan's movement has worked to produce irregularity and undermine access to basic rights for those negatively affected.

However, as we have previously noted, there is also a second problem: even if the Cartagena Declaration had been consistently applied to the Venezuelan context, it is unlikely that all those who had compelling and justifiable reason to flee would have been captured by its categories. For example, a great number of Venezuelans have migrated to Brazil and Colombia since 2016 without, at that time, any sort of special permit that allowed them to stay in the country. Progressively a series of ad hoc permits were established in Brazil, based on the Mercosur Residence Agreement, while Colombia introduced the first Temporary Protection Permit (Permiso Especial de Permanencia, PEP) which allowed some Venezuelans – those who had entered the national territory with a regular immigration status and through an authorized immigration border checkpoint – to stay in the country under some circumstances. Those migrants without documents or the financial means to afford these permits were driven to irregularity or attempted to claim asylum. We explore these normative frameworks further in the next chapter and the gendered implications of these schemes in Chapter 4. Suffice it to say at this point that the form of the expansion of the category of refugeehood exhibited in the Cartagena Declaration reiterates the general problem of a refugee definition based on specifying particular grounds of flight and, hence, inevitably reproduces and politically legitimates the refugee–migrant distinction and the consequent production of a hierarchy of protection for forced migrants (with some being identified as refugees and others not) and thus a political resource for avoiding, minimizing or deflecting responsibilities for those in need of international protection.

Conclusion

At a conceptual and ethical level what is needed to address the problems identified in the preceding discussion is a de-centring of the figure of the refugee as specified by particular grounds of flight and a shift towards a general articulation of the forcibly displaced for whom international protection is needed. We argue that a conceptually appropriate and ethically justifiable articulation is provided in Aleinikoff and Zamore's recent introduction of the category of 'necessary fleer', someone who has compelling reasons to engage in border-crossing movement in order to secure their basic human rights. There are two reasons for proposing this framework, which will be spelt out on detail in Chapter 5, especially when looking at the Latin American context.

First, what are in the 1951 Convention and the wider regional conventions presented as justificatory grounds (such as 'reasonable fear of persecution') that fix the scope of refugeehood are re-situated within the 'necessary fleer' framework as examples of compelling and justifiable reasons for flight that do not limit the potential scope of the category of persons entitled to international protection.[6] The value of this conceptual shift is that it moves us beyond the refugee–migrant distinction and its operation as a political justification for distinguishing among those with compelling and justifiable reasons for border crossing in terms of who is automatically entitled to protection and who is not. As such, the category 'necessary fleer' conceptually disables the political mobilization and exploitation of the refugee–migrant distinction for ideological purposes.

The second reason emerges from reflecting on the potential objection that this shift to the category of 'necessary fleer' simply institutes an alternative categorical divide, that of 'forced' versus 'voluntary' migrants. In one sense, this is right since the category of 'necessary fleer' distinguishes those who have compelling reasons of flight grounded in concern for protection of their basic rights from those who do not have such reasons of practical necessity. But it is important to notice two points about this way of making the distinction. The first is that it avoids tying this distinction to philosophical or legal analyses of, and debates over, the concepts of 'coercion' or 'voluntariness' and instead asks a practical question: 'does this person have compelling reason to seek international protection of their basic rights by engaging in border-crossing movement?'

The second is that the practical question to be addressed refers to 'this person' rather than taking a more general form such as 'does any reasonable person confronted by this type of situation have compelling reason to seek international protection of their basic rights by engaging in border-crossing movement?' The reason that this focus on the first personal viewpoint matters is that the more general form abstracts from the concrete subjectivity of the person concerned, for example, their gender identity, and the specific context of their decision-making. By contrast, the question posed by the necessary fleer framework is intrinsically linked to the embodied and embedded subjectivity of the individual for whom the question of flight arises. Thus, to return to the example with which we concluded Chapter 1, the question of whether pregnant women in Venezuela have compelling reasons for flight is a question that arise for them *as pregnant women* in a particular socio-political context; this is not, of course, to rule out that particular individuals who fall under this description may have other compelling reasons for flight predicated on other dimensions of their subjectivity.

Together these two features of the necessary fleer framework, its combination of *generality* in not tying international protection to specific grounds of flight and *singularity* in taking up the question of flight from the first personal perspective of the agent faced with this question serve to overcome the conceptual and ethical problems posed by the migrant–refugee binary and to disable the political uses of that binary. It thus provides us with a critical framework from which to reflect on the governance of refuge in general and the governance of refuge for Venezuelans in South America in particular, as will be seen in the next chapter.

THREE

Latin American Normative Frameworks of Migration and Asylum

Latin American normative frameworks concerning migration and asylum are generally recognized as 'progressive', 'open' and 'human rights-based' (Brumat and Freier 2020; Brumat and Finn 2021; Zapata and Wenderoth 2021; Hammoud-Gallego and Freier 2022). Experts and commentators have praised Latin America for advancing sustained and 'generous' asylum and refugee policies since the ratification of the 1951 Convention and its 1967 Protocol on the rights of refugees. This appreciation is normally due to progressive, and indeed vernacular, takes on what it means to be a refugee in Latin America. In effect, the region has formally adopted an expanded definition of refugee going beyond the international refugee regime through the regional framework underpinned by the 1984 Cartagena Declaration (Cantor et al 2015: 3). As explored in Chapter 2, Latin America has reinvented boundaries of what it means to be a refugee in the regional context, a process that Cantor calls 'localization' of the international norm on refugees to promote humanitarian and regional cooperation. Interestingly, this expansion took inspiration from the mass displacement experienced in Central America as a consequence of civil wars during the 1980s as the Cold War took hold in Latin America (Cantor 2013). This was written into the Declaration itself: 'in view of the experience gained from the massive flows of refugees in the Central American area, it is necessary to consider enlarging the concept of a refugee'.[1] Indeed, signatory states agreed the existing international refugee system did not provide some groups of forcibly displaced persons in the Americas with the appropriate legal response, rendering it necessary to develop a more appropriate concept to the region's characteristics.

Significantly, the broader definition of refugeehood offered by Cartagena includes not only those who have been individually persecuted, but also those whose lives and liberties were threatened by a series of different circumstances. It therefore did not require a 'subjective' element: a subjective fear of a threat. An objective situation, translated in a factual occurrence, such as, for instance, an armed conflict, was enough to justify international protection under the auspices of regional refugee law.

But it is worth noting that there is actually a long history of protection for people on the move in the Americas that goes back to the backdrop of the 1948 American Declaration of the Rights and Duties of Man, the first international instrument to include the individual right to seek and receive asylum, which later influenced Article 14 of the Universal Declaration on Human Rights itself, with recognition of the same right, and an initiative of Latin American countries. This development inspired the American Convention on Human Rights, which in its Article 22 (7) states that 'every person has the right to seek and be granted asylum in a foreign territory, in accordance with the legislation of the state and international conventions, in the event he is being pursued for political offences or related common crimes'.

In this Latin American context, legal commitments in relation to human rights were developed based on international and regional standards. García (2019) also highlights the role of the Inter-American Human Rights System (IAHRS) and of the regional integration processes establishing jurisprudence in relation to the conditions that ensure the adequate defence of rights, as well as sanctioning processes, in general and with respect to migrants, asylum seekers and refugees in particular. There are also agreements on the recognition of the condition of vulnerability of migrants (IACHR 2003, para. 112; 2010, para. 98; 2012, para. 152) that 'occurs by the mere fact of crossing a border into a state of which the person is not a national and their condition is aggravated or intersected by other variables' (García 2019: 124; also Corte IDH 2020). In this context, the IAHRS guarantees the right to remain and not to be rejected at the border, to *non-refoulement* or expulsion to a country where the life of the individual is in danger (CIDH 2015).

These principles were taken up in the Montevideo Consensus on Population and Development, approved in 2013, and a year later, in the Brazilian Declaration and Plan of Action, wherein participating Latin American countries recognized:

> Developments in the jurisprudence and doctrine of the Inter-American Court of Human Rights, in those countries in which they apply, regarding the content and scope of the right to seek and grant asylum enshrined in the regional human rights instruments, their relationship to international refugee instruments, the jus cogens character of the principle of non-refoulement, including non-rejection at borders and indirect refoulement, and the integration of due process guarantees in refugee status determination procedures, so they are fair and efficient. (Brazilian Declaration 2014: 2)

In addition, the Brazil Plan of Action of 2014 also made commitments to observe the principle of eradication of statelessness in the region and the improvement of cooperation in migratory and asylum matters, including 'social integration' – housing, education and health included – and specific protection to 'vulnerable' groups, such as children and survivors of sexual and gender-based violence (SGBV), demonstrating a holistic view of the challenges and experiences of people on the move in the region. As a result of these developments and goals, the Regional Safe Spaces Network (RSSN) was created 'to facilitate disclosure of SGBV, Child Protection and other serious protection incidents, and ensure access of individuals at risk and survivors to standardized case management and multi-sectorial services along the displacement cycle across countries in the region' (UNHCR 2018b: 89). Its members include national institutions, UN and other international agencies, civil society, and community networks working in five countries in the Americas: Mexico, Guatemala, Costa Rica, Venezuela and Colombia.

Part of this collective duty of securing human rights is creating and sustaining the material and practical conditions of respect for, protection of, and fulfilment of human rights – and it is this which we find articulated not only in human rights treaties but also in SDGs as a key specification of the requirements for states to be able to protect and fulfil the human rights of persons under their jurisdiction.

The goals of the UN 2030 Agenda for Sustainable Development adopted in 2015 added new momentum. Arguably, only one of its 169 targets (target 10.7) across the 17 SDGs addresses migration directly, inviting states to: 'Facilitate orderly, safe, and responsible migration and mobility of people, including through implementation of planned and well-managed migration policies', while other targets make connections to migration topics, including labour migration (8.7 and 8.8), international student mobility (4.b), human trafficking (5.2, 8.7 and 16.2), remittances (10.c), migration data (17.18) and more. But these developments were taken up in the Mesoamerican Comprehensive Development Plan, aiming to make migration a safe option, and to address its root causes in Mexico and the Northern Triangle of Central America (Ventura et al 2021).

Such developments were also included in the Inter-American Principles on the Human Rights of all Migrants, Refugees, Stateless Persons and Victims of Human Trafficking.[2] Focusing particularly on principle 35, regarding health rights, health provision, including sexual and reproductive health, should not depend on migrant status:

> Every migrant has the right to enjoyment of the highest attainable standard of physical and mental health and to the underlying determinants of health; medical attention cannot be denied due to a person's migration status. Health services cannot be denied because of a lack of identity documents. Everyone, regardless of migration status or origin, has the right to receive the same health care as nationals, including sexual and reproductive health and mental health services. States shall take into account the differentiated attention that certain groups require, such as women, children and adolescents.

Engagement with international initiatives to advance and develop refugees and migrants' rights, reception and wellbeing have been particularly welcomed in the case of the *Global Compact on Refugees* (GCR) and the *Global Compact for Safe, Orderly and Regular Migration* (GCM) which enjoyed the massive participation of Latin American countries. In the GCR, for instance, almost all Latin American and Caribbean countries (with the notable exclusion of Cuba) made extensive pledges deriving from the compact. Brazil's government made 11 different pledges, the majority of which involved involve Venezuelan migration, while Colombia's pledges mostly involved the combat of statelessness, especially concerning children born in the country from Venezuelan parents. With 24 pledges, Mexico highlighted its goal at guaranteeing free universal healthcare for migrants in transit and permanent residents in the country, and Peru pledged to guarantee effective and equal access to rights to asylum seekers it hosts. However, few or no pledges with regards to gender-responsive policies and laws to refugees have been made by Latin American governments.

Treaties, guidelines, principles, compacts, pledges, and declarations thus comprise the mixed variety of elements, either mandatory or not, that form the normative framework for migrants and refugees in Latin America, which underwrite worldwide perception of its progressiveness, especially in comparison to regions with more restrictive frameworks (Mármora 2010; Acosta 2018). Brumat and Finn (2021) highlight how norms of free residence, equal rights, the explicit mentioning of the 'right to migrate', and non-criminalization of migration, feature in many South American frameworks, and supported the regional Residence Agreement of Mercosur (RAM) under the auspices of Mercosur whose members include Brazil, Argentina, Paraguay and Uruguay, and associated countries Chile, Colombia, Peru, Bolivia and Ecuador. Venezuela did not sign the RAM and has been a suspended member of Mercosur since late 2016, so its nationals cannot access this 'subregional residency'. To a large extent, the subregional regime, alongside other normative and national developments, have made the irregular–regular migration or refugee–migrant binaries irrelevant, if not de jure, de facto protection to all migrants (Zapata and Prieto Rosas 2020). Brazil, Argentina, Chile, Ecuador, Peru and Uruguay, for instance, do not formally make a distinction in their laws between refugees and asylum seekers regarding the access to formal employment and permits (Asylum Access 2018). Regarding the right to health, Brazil's constitution and Argentina's laws determine universal access to free healthcare services regardless of migratory status.

Indeed, despite their differences, the developments towards more progressive, liberal or human rights-based frameworks for migrants and specifically forced migrants in the region and subregion are noteworthy. All of this serves to suggest that Latin America – and particularly South America – is well-placed to respond to events such as the Venezuela exodus in ways that respect the key principles of protection outlined within the necessary fleer framework:

1. *Safety*: enabling those in need to access a safe place.
2. *Rebuilding Lives and Communities: Enjoyment of Asylum*: inclusion through rights and freedom, or as we would put it, the opportunity to live in and with dignity.
3. *Solution*: being in a secure position with one's rights protected, where this is pragmatically likely to include enjoyment of, or access to, a membership status.
4. *Mobility*: being entitled to seek protection, move with states of asylum, and have opportunities to travel to other states of asylum.
5. *Voice*: being entitled to voice concerning how they are governed through the international protection regime and in their contexts of asylum.

As we will see, however, the lived experience of necessary fleers from Venezuela does not exhibit the application of these principles within either the region or the specific states in which they are situated. Rather than a principled rights-based approach to the challenges of international protection, we find a series of more or less generous, more or less restrictive, ad hoc measures predicated on the use of discretionary executive powers. Rather than a rule-based framework that guides and coordinates local, national, regional and international responses, the practical actuality of the experience of Venezuelan necessary fleers more closely resembles a limited and restricted 'care and maintenance' system. Our analysis in this chapter will show the vast gap between the promise of the legal framework represented in claims of de facto protection to all forced migrants and the practical reality confronted by Venezuela necessary fleers.

The protection gap and the return of the migrant–refugee binary

Despite many progressive developments in relation to migration and refugee laws in the region, the retreat of its 'pink tide' phase and a turn to more restrictive and right-wing governments, combined with the massive displacement of Venezuelans, have posed a real challenge to the region's migration and asylum frameworks. As we noted in Chapter 2, although the region has seen the widespread adoption, fully or partially, into domestic laws of the Cartagena Declaration, it is still underused in practice. This was identified as one of the main issues for the region's protection regime in the triennial progress report of the 2014 Brazil Plan of Action (UNHCR 2018b).

Venezuelans in particular have been affected by a restrictive turn, with almost no countries recognizing them as refugees under the Cartagena Declaration, despite being urged to do so by the UNHCR. In fact, in the 2020 Global Report, UNHCR introduced a new category of 'Venezuelans displaced abroad' to refer to the forced displacement of Venezuelans in Latin America. According to the agency, such classification related to 'persons of Venezuelan origin who are likely to be in need of international protection under the criteria contained in the Cartagena Declaration, but who have not applied for asylum in the country in which they are present' (UNHCR 2022).[3] Thus, as we noted in Chapter 1, Venezuelans could be classified as refugees, asylum seekers or merely 'displaced abroad', all of which highlight their forced movement, but also demonstrate the uncertainty and fluidity of their official status throughout the region and in the world. Such 'categorial crossroads' and consequent uncertainty generated criticism from the Venezuelan activist Ligia Bolivar (2020) who commented that 'Venezuelans now are not refugees, nor asylum seekers, displaced persons, persons of concern, stateless persons, or returnees. We are not even "people in a refugee-like situation". We are a new fauna called Venezuelans displaced abroad'.

The failure to use the Cartagena Declaration regarding Venezuelans was compounded by more restrictive institutional responses to this rapid increase in intraregional mobility. Although some claim Venezuelans had 'open borders', even if informally (Brumat and Freier 2020), this claim is undermined by the fact that Venezuelans have had to engage in irregular border crossing and undocumented migration confronting all the risks and challenges that come along with irregular movement. Indeed, attitudes to the reception of Venezuelans throughout the region shifted quickly, amid rising levels of xenophobia, increasing entry restrictions, militarization and border closures, as well as mass expulsions (Zapata and Prieto Rosas 2020). Without asylum recognition for Venezuelans, some countries, such as Peru and Chile, created ad hoc legal migratory regularization permits, for which they have been globally praised. However, as displacement increased, they started to require visas and a stronger documentational threshold at border sites. In 2019, for instance, Peru required Venezuelans to have both a 'humanitarian' visa and a passport (at least an expired one) to enter the country. High costs, waiting periods and bureaucratic difficulties meant that Venezuelans would be deterred from migrating regularly and safely to Peru, and would either migrate irregularly or would be immobilized in Venezuela enduring the risks involved in remaining in a country undergoing a humanitarian crisis. Even when Peruvian courts ruled in 2018 that it was illegal to require a passport to apply for a temporary resident permit (Permiso Temporal de Permanencia, or PTP), because this would essentially restrict free movement, the Peruvian government led a backlash against this judgment with then President Vizcarra announcing a time limit to enter the country to apply for the PTP (Bauer 2021). This would further restrict access to rights, increase dangers and risks in displacement, and enhance legal insecurity for Venezuelans.

Similarly, Chile created so-called 'democratic responsibility visas', which were also required for entry to Venezuelans, who had to apply in Chilean consulate posts abroad. Requiring passports (even if expired), criminal records and the payment of US$30, this meant many, if not most, Venezuelans would be unable to access the visa's threshold, either because they could not afford the costs or because they do not have the necessary documents and cannot obtain them (Doña-Reveco 2022)

Relatedly, in 2018 and 2019, Ecuador issued a series of reforms which closed the border to many and restricted the possibility for undocumented migrants to regularize. Efforts to require passports for Venezuelans to enter the country were blocked by Ecuadorian courts but demonstrated the country's goal of curbing Venezuelan migration. Such measures were further increased with executive decrees which required Venezuelans to show their negative criminal records, effectively impeding their regular entry, transit and stay (Selee et al 2019; Bauer 2021), considering the difficulty in obtaining them. As with Chile and Peru, Ecuador also issued visas that offered temporary stays for Venezuelans, but their costs were so high that the majority of vulnerable and poor Venezuelan migrants were effectively prevented from regularizing their status through this measure.

Overall, these temporary permits and visas were ad hoc exceptional measures under the guise of progressive and seemingly welcoming 'humanitarian' responses, yet ultimately avoiding recognizing Venezuelan fleers as refugees under the Cartagena Declaration. Furthermore, most of these ad hoc measures were executive-mandated allowing governments to shape migratory decision-making through bureaucratic requirements opening or restricting Venezuelan mobility at will, without actually shifting policy towards greater mobility rights, entry and regularization in response to necessary fleers.

Moreover, the variety of migratory statuses, either as 'temporary migrant', 'permanent migrant', with 'humanitarian permit', 'Venezuelan displaced abroad', 'asylum seeker', 'refugee' and 'undocumented migrant', also meant different access to fundamental rights of protection, health coverage and access social protection schemes (Vera Espinoza et al 2021). Pierola and Rodriguez (2020: 5) argue there is a great disparity between nationals and non-nationals' affiliation to healthcare systems in Latin America, as is the case in Colombia in 2019, for example, with only 27 per cent of migrants affiliated to the Colombian health system, whereas 94 per cent of nationals had such access.

In most cases, migrants face barriers associated to legal status that affect access and use of health services including lack of information and/or documentation, fear of deportation, discrimination, language and cultural barriers (Obach et al 2020; Liberona and Mansilla 2017; Carreño-Calderón et al 2020; Zambrano-Barragán et al 2021; UNHCR 2021). Other legal-bureaucratic barriers relate to health governance and the implementation of policy by local authorities (Bengochea et al 2020) or, like in Ecuador, being able to afford the appropriate health insurance documents that allow access to free basic healthcare (Malo 2020).

In short, although Latin America, and South America particularly, do have 'progressive' or 'liberal' normative frameworks, especially in comparison to the more restrictive systems operative in most of the Global North and much of Africa, these frameworks do not act effectively to secure the protection or rights of necessary fleers in general. In many instances, as we have seen, the refusal to apply asylum frameworks to Venezuelans reproduces the problems of the migrant–refugee binary discussed in Chapter 2, showcasing the negative outcomes of ad hoc temporary and flexible permits and visas, which prioritize government interests rather than the rights of displaced peoples. In many cases, the various bureaucratic requirements of such visas and permits effectively push women towards irregular journeys and with it risks to health and safety, generating irregularity and other violations of the rights of (forced) migrants. Despite the legal frameworks of many countries not requiring regular migrant status to access certain basic rights, such as the right to health and to safe and regular employment, the lived realities of migrants' experiences, especially undocumented migrants, challenges claims that there is de facto protection to *all* migrants in South America. Indeed, rather than a picture of dignity in displacement, what are disclosed are significantly limited forms of 'respect as observance' with access to basic rights too often dependent on discretionary executive power and a serious lack of 'respect as respectfulness' exhibited in failures to engage with the voices of the displaced and increasingly level of xenophobia towards them. This has been particularly seen during the COVID-19 pandemic as the previously 'open' borders in South America faced an unprecedented regional closure, and regular migration was halted with migrants stigmatized as disease carriers. This greatly impacted the character of Venezuelans' movement in the region, whether fleeing or returning to Venezuela or looking to move from their country of temporary settlement to another state in the region because of, for example, discriminatory policies, and their relative inability to enjoy equal access to labour markets, housing and healthcare, these being further negatively impacted by the pandemic (Bengochea et al 2020). We explore these points further in the following section through two cases that particularly stand out: the national responses to Venezuelan displacement of Colombia and of Brazil.

Local frameworks and responses

Brazil

Until Venezuelans started fleeing to Brazil, the country's reception of migrants was modest. Migrants were mostly intraregional applying for residency under the RAM. Forced migrants were mostly Sub-Saharan Africans and Syrians, whose numbers did not reach the tens of thousands, and Haitians, which had the biggest numbers of entries the country had witnessed until 2015 – reported to be at over 60,000 by then. With a 307 per cent increase in asylum requests from Venezuelans in 2016 compared to 2015, and more than 330,000 Venezuelan displaced in the country by 2022,[4] it is no surprise that an exceptional migration pattern led to unprecedented responses in Brazil.

In November 2017, the new Brazilian migration law abandoned the framework of the 'Alien's Statute of 1980' created under military rule, and introduced a new set of principles that underscored migration policies on a human rights basis. The 2017 Migration Law privileged the non-criminalization of migration, humanitarian assistance, promoted equal access of migrants to social programmes, as well as migratory regularization, established clear rules to limit forced removal powers, including rejection of collective deportations. It was an unparalleled legal achievement and policy response to the increasing numbers of Venezuelans arriving.

The immigration and asylum structure of Brazilian law has reproduced a binary model that divides governance of migration by assigned migratory categories, that is, asylum and 'economic' migration. CONARE is responsible for the former; the Brazilian National Immigration Council for the latter. After an initial restrictive response to incoming Venezuelans in 2016, with multiple accounts of collective deportations (G1 Roraima 2016) and in particular local rejection of incoming migrants, the Brazilian National Immigration Council decreed an ad hoc temporary permit for Venezuelans. As such, although the majority of Venezuelans were applying for asylum, the initial response of the two administrative bodies responsible for immigration and asylum governance was to try and contain Venezuelan flows under the 'immigration', rather than the 'asylum', framework. Venezuelans who applied for the two-year residency permit had to choose between it and their asylum claim without receiving the necessary legal guidance of the consequences of this choice. Furthermore, its strict requirements, including presentation of a valid passport and other documents, meant that even the residency was limited to a small proportion of Venezuelans, the majority of whom remained solely as asylum seekers. Considering the context of its creation and the requirements to abandon asylum claims, granting residency seemed a deliberate attempt to move the focus of governance of Venezuelan mobility away from the 'refugee label' (Zetter 2007).

Although the Brazilian Refugee Law of 1997 has been globally praised for its 'progressiveness', CONARE, the organization which applies it and creates asylum policies in the country, has received criticism for its restrictive and conservative interpretation and application of the law (see Tinker and Sartoretto 2018), including (and mostly because of) its lack of use of the Cartagena Declaration. The deliberate attempt to switch Venezuelan migration from the 'refugee' to the 'migrant' label through residency permits, and without a clear decision on whether or not the situation in Venezuela fell under one of the legal possibilities of refugeehood, was legally enforced in 2018 through another decree. That decree in turn decreased the number of documents required, established a fee waiver for migrants who could not afford it, and opened the possibility of turning permits into permanent residency after two years, if the migrants showed minimum means to support themselves.

This was indeed a huge improvement; one that came at a time when a great number of Venezuelan fleers were applying for asylum, creating not only backlogs but a political and economic challenge for the state. However, it also meant that Venezuelans, not always legally supported and well informed, had to make a 'choice' as to whether renounce asylum claims in order to benefit from available pathways to regularization. As Zapata and Wenderoth (2021) claim, with refugee status, Venezuelans have international protection, a more secure system of social protection and integration, greater rights to family reunification and are more robustly protected from refoulement. This meant that although an ad hoc residency status and refugee status were being used as equal frameworks for protection, they implied a different set of national, regional and international frameworks with distinctive sets of rights, which Venezuelan fleers were unaware of when having to make such 'choice'.

In June 2019, the Brazilian government classified Venezuela as a country in a situation of 'serious and generalized violation of human rights', which opened a legal pathway for migrants to be accepted as refugees. Even this welcomed decision to recognize Venezuelans prima facie as refugees in 2019 under the auspices of the Cartagena Declaration was determined politically, in a context wherein the newly elected far-right president Jair Bolsonaro used this decision as an ideological tool to legitimate his style of rule and to counter the legitimacy claims of Maduro's government in Venezuela (Tavares and Cabral 2020). The positive reception of this decision should not overshadow the years of categorical or labelling transitions Venezuelans went through before this, and the governance of migration under a categorial hierarchy, which placed refugeehood as the most privileged, and least accessible, one (Zetter 2007). Indeed, the Brazilian government made deliberate attempts to restrain Venezuelans from claiming refugee status and, when unsuccessful, made tens of thousands of them wait years for a decision. That this led to a positive outcome for migrants themselves was a matter of political luck rather than the product of a rule-based system aimed at securing rights.

The discretionary governance of Venezuelan mobility was heightened during the outbreak of COVID-19 pandemic. Brazil not only left, at President Bolsonaro's orders, the *Global Compact for Safe, Regular and Orderly Migration*, but also issued executive decrees that created the category of 'dangerous migrant' (Provisional Measure n. 666/2019) which changed rules involving border refusals and forced removals, giving more discretion to border police, and effectively criminalizing certain migrants, something which went directly against the *ethos* that the new, human rights-based, migratory law Brazil had introduced in 2017. This was the backdrop of a restrictive and discriminatory policy that was introduced during the COVID-19 pandemic. In 2020 and 2021, just a few months after Brazil was praised for its recognition of Venezuelans as refugees and the humanitarian structure created, the country closed its borders on March 2020, as did many states in South

America, using as justification the need to contain the spread of the virus. Closing borders not only ran against WHO advice under current International Health Regulations but had serious effects on the ability to deliver medical (and other) aid and technical support to address the coronavirus. The health of migrants and people on the move not only suffered because of the virus but also due to the intended and unintended effects of the travel restrictions, including many individuals, particularly displaced populations, facing neglectful and discriminatory treatment. As explained in detail in Chapter 4, the prohibition of (regular) entry to all Venezuelans, essentially *created* irregular displacement and entry, and with it risks and vulnerabilities that had significant gendered effects on women and girl fleers which seriously affected their sexual and reproductive health, and access to protection and healthcare to mitigate them. Once in the country, presidential decrees prohibited regularization and asylum claims by irregular migrants, which meant tens of thousands of Venezuelans became undocumented for almost two years in Brazil. This has given rise to significant protection gaps.

The different and hierarchical levels of protection pre-pandemic and the levels of irregularity among Venezuelans during the COVID-19 pandemic undermine the basis of de facto protection regardless of migrant status. This is especially the case when looking at access to both mobility rights and the right to health. In the case of mobility rights, there is a clear de jure difference between being an asylum seeker/refugee, being a migrant with an ad hoc temporary permit, and being undocumented. First, regarding the right to *seek* protection, the IAHRS has a strong protection framework, and such a *right* should be protected even amid exceptional circumstances, such as during pandemics, along with the protection from return in the cases of those whose life, freedom or wellbeing could be thereby put in danger. In practice, however, several collective deportations happened to mostly irregular Venezuelan fleers in 2016 in clear violation of the broader protection from *non-refoulement*. Such experience established a clear hierarchy allowing access to the right to claim asylum only to some. However, as many women we interviewed reported, at the border police demanded documents from the children, such as valid passports, along with approvals from the other parent, something most of these women did not have and typically could not obtain. These women and children would be barred from entry and would have to cross without authorization or turn back, regardless of their motives for fleeing their country, their vulnerability or the increased protection given to children by the IAHRS (as noted earlier).

For those 'regular' migrants and fleers in settlement, legal and bureaucratic restrictions were also evident. Although access to health services in Brazil is free and universal for all regardless of nationality or status, according to the country's federal constitution, Roraima's governor decreed in 2016 a state-wide 'state of (health) emergency' due to local health services, particularly hospitals, being overloaded following the inflows of displaced Venezuelans (Brandão 2016). In 2018, the state of Roraima attempted to create bureaucratic restrictions on migrants' access to public services, demanding the closure of the Venezuela–Brazil border due to increasing levels of alleged criminality and, among other reasons, overload of the health and education systems, in addition to the risk of epidemics (Cintra 2020). The restrictive response was also seen in a local decree issued in August 2018, which required migrants to show their passports to access local health services. Documentation was one of the main devices which local actors used to limit and restrict forced migrants from having access to health services and rights, which particularly affected undocumented migrants – legal status distinctively impacts migrants' access to protection (Zapata 2021).

This was politically unsurprising, and a consequence of fleers of necessity reaching and settling in border areas that are already suffering entrenched socioeconomic problems and uneven development. Venezuelans mostly migrated and remained in the northern-most states of Brazil, Roraima and Amazonas, closest to the Brazil–Venezuela border, and among Brazil's poorest states, with little resources to respond to the increasing pressures on local services. By 2018 10 per cent of the population in Roraima was estimated to be Venezuelan migrants (Doocy et al 2019). As we explore in Chapter 4, Brazil's response to these demands was the creation of a federal inter-agency operation involving the Armed Forces, government services, NGOs and international organizations in order to provide support for local governments through what was called 'Operation Welcome' (*Operação Acolhida*, in Portuguese). This initiative had a threefold focus: to control and order the border; to create, manage and allocate migrants to shelters; and to improve the capability of local health provision (Moulin and Magalhães 2020).

Such an achievement has had many positive impacts on local availability of services and access to basic socioeconomic rights for incoming migrants after its implementation in 2018. However, as borders closed, so did Operation Welcome's reception to irregular migrants, at least at first, with reports that undocumented Venezuelan migrants were gathered in front of Boa Vista bus station, essentially homeless and sleeping rough, because they were not accepted under Operation Welcome's structure. Several vulnerable migrants were forcibly removed from Operation Welcome shelters and deported to Venezuela.[5]

Once the border was opened, immigration frameworks were restored yet human rights-based asylum and migration policies co-existed with contradictions of policy and implementation that manifested as barriers to the exercise of rights in general and determinants of unmet sexual and reproductive health in particular, reproducing gendered inequalities for forcibly displaced women and girls.

Colombia

The Colombian case is the other important case study in understanding responses to Venezuelan forced migration. As the country hosting the majority of Venezuelan displaced in the world and in South America, its response determines how the largest number of necessary fleers are being treated in the region. Colombia is quite new as a refugee/migrant hosting state: until the Venezuelan inflows, the country was mainly a 'producer' of refugees (with many going to Venezuela), occasionally being a place of transit for internationally displaced individuals. This may be one of the reasons why Colombia has been fairly limited in its application of the Cartagena Declaration: it has few recognized refugees, only 320, 30 per cent of which are Venezuelans, an insignificant number, considering the approximately 1.7 million Venezuelans currently in the country (UNHCR 2019). In other words, the country has no 'culture of asylum', despite having ratified the 1951 Convention and the 1967 Protocol, as well as integrating the Cartagena Declaration into its national framework (Decree n. 2840/2013). Despite the decision to not recognize Venezuelans as refugees, Colombia, along with Argentina, Brazil, Chile, Costa Rica, the Dominican Republic, Ecuador, Guyana, Paraguay and Peru, declared, in the Quito Process, that the situation in Venezuela had reached levels in which it undermined protection and respect for human rights (Freier et al 2020). Indeed, not many Venezuelans currently in Colombia have applied for asylum – a little less than 10,000. This could be explained by the unlikelihood of a timely and positive decision, the prohibition against asylum seekers working or having access to state-sponsored healthcare, the desire to engage in pendular migration (routinely return to Venezuela, prohibited for those with refugee status), among other reasons. Such poor access to socioeconomic rights as an asylum seeker with no parallel state aid during the asylum process makes it very unattractive for Venezuelans.

Moreover, the Colombian government has issued a series of ad hoc, temporary permits to Venezuelans (*Permiso Especial de Permanencia*, PEP), which are free, fast and easy to access, making it a more enticing option to displaced Venezuelans.

The use of these permits in the Colombian response to Venezuelan displacement were internationally praised and, overall, the Colombian government's public discourses have always revolved around their humanitarian commitment towards Venezuelans (Restrepo et al 2018). Despite that, the Cartagena Declaration's enlarged concept of refugee could have provided the Colombian government with a way of creating a legal pathway for incoming Venezuelans with a range of rights under international, regional and national refugee law frameworks. Had they used it and put in place the administrative systems required to process asylum claims in a timely manner (for example, by using group-based criteria), there would be no need to create from scratch a responsive system to the massive inflows of Venezuelans based on PEPs. Indeed, although some authors claim that Colombia 'opted to forgo the distinction between refugees and migrants' (Selee and Bolter 2022), it can also be claimed that by opting to *not* implement asylum as a legal pathway to Venezuelans in the country, the binary distinction was upheld by default and it also managed to avoid public and political perceptions of incentivizing inflows through refugee support (Del Real 2022; Selee et al 2019). As a consequence, asylum in Colombia has been at best irrelevant, as very few Venezuelans have been recognized as refugees, and at worst a barrier to protection.

To a large extent, PEPs were issued to solve past irregularity, giving the opportunity to Venezuelan migrants to apply for it within a limited timeframe, subject to possession of a valid passport along with evidence relating to lack of criminal records. With such a high evidential and documentational threshold, Venezuelans who arrived past a certain date, those who had crossed the border irregularly and had no way to attest their date of entry, and those without evidence concerning lack of criminal records would remain undocumented. In May 2021, a new regularization scheme, the *Estatuto Temporal de Protección para Migrantes Venezolanos* (or ETPV, short for Temporary Protection Statute for Venezuelan Migrants), was issued by then Colombian President Iván Duque. Although this gave an institutional answer for the regularization of very large numbers of Venezuelans, the ETPV required that Venezuelan migrants and asylum seekers fulfilled certain eligibility criteria, targeting Venezuelans in irregular migratory status, who have entered the country before 31st January 2021; or Venezuelans who have entered Colombia through an official checkpoint since then. This arbitrary cut-off date meant that not all Venezuelan migrants have been eligible to apply; and, by 2022, over 310,000 remained irregular (R4V 2023). Furthermore, Del Real (2022) claimed that these schemes that were created for undocumented migrants without valid passports, often were not widely publicized, resulted in a low rate of success and access. In these cases, it may seem actions and decisions were issued *in order to fail*.

Irregular/regular status is therefore a by-product of the country's responses to the massive inflows of Venezuelan displaced persons. If legal status, in turn, affects access to basic human rights, Colombia could be an example of well-intentioned humanitarian, welcoming policies that set problematic precedents concerning who is treated with humanity and who is not. Furthermore, Del Real (2022) characterizes Colombian management of Venezuelan flows under a 'liminal legality' framework, wherein there is some sort of legal protection, but its scope is blurred, with no clear pathway to permanent residency or citizenship, and with renewals highly dependent on executive discretion. As such, even the 2021 ETPV, highly acclaimed worldwide, is not sufficient to overcome the production of irregularity and still generates exclusions among Venezuelan migrants. This is because, in order to be eligible to apply for the ETPV, migrants must be already recipients of previous PEPs, or in the case of undocumented Venezuelans, they must be able to prove they were in Colombia before 31 January 2021. Venezuelans who enter the country between 29 May 2021 and 28 May 2023 through the official border checkpoints and stamp their passports can also access the ETPV. Moreover, PEP holders must register for a census and are only then eligible for the ten-year residency. The various types of requirements mean many migrants will remain undocumented, and future ones might become irregular due to the policy's constraints. And, as argued by Seele et al (2019) and Del Real (2022), with no direct pathway to permanency or citizenship, and with the high level of discretion around these measures, it may very well be that many more necessary fleers become undocumented.

The production of irregularity through highly discretionary policies also reflects a rights-exclusionary approach that affects almost all Venezuelans. Vulnerable migrants and those with the least resources are impacted the most and their already poor socioeconomic conditions are compounded due to how migrant status affects access to basic rights, particularly the right to health and the right to labour. In Colombia, undocumented migrants do not have access to formal employment or labour rights, and only have access to emergency health services, while migrants with a valid legal status have full access. Even access to emergency services is strictly limited to:

> 1) those facing life-threatening emergencies and arriving in emergency rooms at public hospitals; 2) those facing urgent maternity needs and immediate pregnancy needs; 3) children, especially infants, with neonatal, developmental, and immunization needs. Other segments of migrant populations – older adults, men, non-pregnant women – and other categories of health issues – chronic disease, non-life-threatening conditions, and mental health – are not covered. (Zambrano-Barragán et al 2021: 3)

This leaves many forced migrants essentially rightless. If they wish to be seen by medical professionals, they must pay – but without formal employment for irregular migrants (or even asylum seekers), it is unlikely migrants will be able to afford the costs. This explains why less than 22 per cent of migrants have full access to healthcare services in the country (Profamilia 2020). Other everyday barriers, such as economic insecurity and discrimination, affect access to health services and rights and are greater among the undocumented, something which was worsened during the pandemic (Zambrano-Barragán et al 2021). Even availability of the COVID-19 vaccine was initially announced to be restricted to nationals and non-nationals with some sort of legal status, undocumented ones excluded – though this later changed as vaccines became more widespread (Bowser et al 2022).

All these examples demonstrate wide gaps between seemingly positive laws for migrants and refugees, and the lived experiences of forced migrants themselves. The importance of Colombia as a case study beyond the numbers of Venezuelans situated within its borders is that it demonstrates how a positive, pro-immigration discourse combined with some real achievements through the use of ad hoc regularization can coexist with exclusionary policies and discretionary power (Acosta and Freier 2015) operating through 'migrant' statuses rather than 'refugee' status. As such, it is normally the most vulnerable migrants who become irregular migrants, and their irregularity further compounds their vulnerabilities, by prohibiting or limiting access to the basic rights such as healthcare and labour rights. Rather than de facto protection for *all* migrants, regardless of status, analysis of lived experiences of mobility and socioeconomic rights demonstrate de facto rightlessness for undocumented Venezuelan migrants (and asylum seekers) in Colombia, and liminal legality and legal uncertainty for those with some sort of migrant, but not refugee, status.

Conclusion

Latin America is globally known for its progressive stance on migration and asylum, with important achievements in regional, subregional and national legal frameworks. Venezuelan necessary fleers are thus an important case, given the unprecedented nature of such mobility levels in the region and their location in neighbouring South American countries, for reflecting on the protection gaps that emerge between the promise of such frameworks and the actuality to which necessary fleers are exposed. Analysis of legal frameworks and policies at the regional and national levels, although important to understand the range of rights formally available for forced migrants in the region is not sufficient to address the reality of protection regimes on the ground as our analysis of how Brazil and Colombia have managed the inflows of displaced Venezuelans illustrates.

In the case of Brazil, an impressive structure of protection, combined with progressive frameworks, proved, on the one hand, to be extremely flawed in the everyday and localized experiences of rights of Venezuelan fleers and, on the other, to instantiate a highly discretionary mode of executive governance. Documentation requirements were used in various different ways to restrict the access of Venezuelans to Brazilian territory, to limit their access to healthcare services and to formal employment, as well as other socioeconomic rights, despite such requirements having no place in the highly progressive formal legal frameworks of this country.

In the Colombian case, all the regularizations made available to Venezuelans were not enough to curb irregularity, even the initiative to give a ten-year residency to them, with just under 60 per cent of Venezuelans still undocumented in that country (Welsh 2021). The highly praised solutions to Venezuelan documentational issues in the country are not as durable and sustainable as they appear to be on paper, and their *liminal legality* means Venezuelans are exposed to highly discretionary governmental measures, rather than having their rights secured within a rule-based structure of protection.

Both of these cases, as well as the wider regional responses sketched at the start of this chapter, demonstrate how protection gaps are produced through de facto hierarchies of rights, and arbitrary decisions about deservingness and protection. It is not our aim to condemn Colombia, Brazil or the other states in the region for the measures that they have taken nor to deny the real achievements made under highly constrained circumstances (we will turn to issues of responsibility in Chapter 5). Rather our focus is on drawing attention to:

1. the ways in which a secure regime of protection for necessary fleers is disabled by recourse to forms of migration governance based on the discretionary use of executive powers in ways that are highly consequential for the forced migration–gender–health nexus, and
2. the necessity of the analysis of protection regimes to dig down to their operation on the ground rather than staying at the level of general rights endorsed in constitutional, regional or international law.

In this chapter, our focus has been on demonstrating how diverse migration statuses affect and shape access to rights, and how the mode of migration governance can make the enjoyment of rights precarious by not grounding it securely in a rules-based framework. Yet the deployment of ad hoc executive governance in special visas and residents permits that produced irregularity for many Venezuelans also enabled xenophobia and other forms of non-responsiveness to displaced women especially in disadvantaged border areas where many Venezuelans were situated. This, in turn, affected their access to healthcare and health rights. To demonstrate and explore the character of this effect, we turn in the next chapter to the voices of the displaced women themselves.

FOUR

Protecting the Human Right to Health of Women and Girls from Venezuela as Necessary Fleers

When women and girls reach their countries of destination, issues of documentation matter, both in how they experience their (health) rights in their everyday circumstances, but also in how they perceive themselves and are socially perceived as rights-holders. Even in contexts where documentation does not seem to be a problem for accessing basic rights, such as healthcare, women can be 'socially undocumented'. According to Amy Reed-Sandoval (2020: 36), 'socially undocumented identity is an ethno-racial and class identity, and the social group of socially undocumented people includes people with and without legal authorization to live in the country where they currently reside'. This means that whether necessary fleers are documented or not, gender, race, ethnicity and class can intersect with their migrant status in affecting their everyday experiences of rights as they are socially seen or thought of as undocumented. Everyday barriers associated with social perceptions and practices can affect women fleers' enjoyment of rights independent of status. This is not to argue that documentation does not matter. Chapter 3 showed how documentation is used in migratory governance to make access to rights more or less difficult. This chapter will argue that, additionally, inequalities and injustices rise from intersecting variables, including gender, regardless of status. In other words, documentation matters for Venezuelans in the contexts analysed, but everyday *gendered* social experiences of rights are key in unfolding the importance of going beyond issues of documentation and status.

What will become clear is that displaced women and girls have their access to rights and dignity severely curtailed. One gender-sensitive area where this becomes apparent is in relation to sexual and reproductive health (SRH). SRH represents one of the bleakest experiences of gendered harms that affect women and girls' rights, dignity and freedoms during displacement and beyond. Yet gender-sensitive systems of protection to address the challenges of sexual and reproductive health of women and girls in displacement are not always available, effective or willing to respond appropriately in upholding protection for all migrants.

In this chapter we focus attention on displaced women and girls as necessary fleers in order to detail the ways in which their experience of displacement shapes their SRH and access to SRH rights. We develop this chapter based on the many interviews and discussions we had during fieldwork, giving voice to displaced women and girls. It contextualizes this discussion with the framework of the human right to health and aims to articulate the rights to which displaced women and girls are entitled and the terms on which they can exercise these rights as requirements of dignity. It then analyses whether existing protection systems at regional and national levels are implemented in the cases of Colombia and Brazil in responding to Venezuelan female migrants. The chapter addresses gendered needs regarding the SRH of women and the responsibilities of states to provide protection. It evaluates implementation across the range of refugee and migrant statuses in terms of whether they address the protection needs of the female mobile population and their rights relating to SRH. A focused discussion is offered regarding forced migration as a determinant of health, highlighting the lack of adequate infrastructures and policies needed to break cycles of deprivation and exclusion specifically affecting displaced women and girls. The chapter also discusses the inadequacy of protection frameworks for displaced women and the relationship of this protection gap to the ways in which responsibility for displaced women is allocated.

Women and girls as necessary fleers

Venezuelan migrant women are necessary fleers, whose drivers of forced displacement have been reasons of practical necessity, ranging from hunger to gender-based violence to fear of dying in childbirth. Of the total of Venezuelans displaced, just under half are women and girls. A study led by Fiocruz Foundation shows that, out of 2,012 Venezuelan migrant women and adolescent girls interviewed in Manaus and Boa Vista, Brazil, who were asked what their main reasons for flight were (with the option of listing more than one reason), they responded as follows: 54 per cent highlighted reasons relating to difficulties in obtaining food; 37.8 per cent stressed reasons relating to access to health treatments, while 27.3 per cent listed reasons related to gender-based violence and a similar percentage reasons based on seeking work (Do Carmo Leal et al 2022). These are people who may reasonably feel that they have no alternative other than to leave the country and enter a migration process because of direct threats or the prospects of physical insecurity or the loss of shelter and livelihood, or because their ability to care for themselves and their families are radically undermined. As put by Myrza, a 33-year-old female Venezuelan migrant, who migrated to Brazil in 2018: "I decided to migrate because the situation was very extreme. I no longer had a job, the situation was precarious, and I was in great need, very hungry … I could not return to Venezuela because returning means going back to need and hunger" (Manaus, 30 June 2021).

Likewise, a 39-year-old female migrant who left Venezuela in 2016, stated:

> 'The crisis made me leave, looking for an improvement, to be able to help my family. My family stayed there, my

> mother, my brothers, my cousins. … I was sick too. I also left because of that, because I needed an operation. And there in Venezuela, time was passing by and I had no help. … That is my main reason … I was told that here they could operate quickly.' (Marcela, Manaus, 8 June 2021)

Finally, a 19-year-old migrant summarized a common experience of necessity as follows: "Sometimes if we bought food we couldn't buy clothes, or if we bought clothes, we didn't buy food. … And then we decided that the one who was leaving was me" (Eva, 13 July 2021). Migration for many of them is also part of the responsibility assumed by women in their mothering and caregiving roles:

> 'I had to emigrate for my children, for a better future for them, for a better education … I have three children, I had to leave two, and I only brought one, to be able to work. Since I can't leave them with a stranger here. Well, I'll keep fighting to give them a better future and when established I'll go and get them. And well, that's my story. … A lot of sadness because I don't have my other two.' (Flaka, Manaus, 2 October 2021)

This is echoed in many stories of (gendered) necessity and responsibility. Nancy fled to Colombia in 2020 because of her children, "because I could not even provide the basic needs. … Sometimes they did not eat or I stopped eating to give the food to my children, do you understand me?" (Bogotá, 7 October 2021).

Stories of necessity are all too common drivers of forced migration. What the situations of Venezuelan women demonstrate is that gender impacts and broadens strict and binary understandings of what counts as drivers of forced displacement, as seen in Chapter 2. Particularly, what Venezuelan women showcase in their narratives is that healthcare and sexual and reproductive rights are basic human rights that violation of (for them and for those they care for) counts as a compelling reason for (forcibly) migrating. In situations of displacement, and forced displacement in particular, women and girls' vulnerabilities and needs are heightened by precarious paths and dangerous crossings, inadequate access to food and water, long walks, traumatic situations experienced heightened by risks of sexual violence. Migrant women and girls, particularly those travelling by irregular paths, might not have had access to medical attention or treatment before or during their travel and on arrival accessing and negotiating sexual and reproductive health services could be a complex and conflicting experience – all of which can be exacerbated by inadequate access to healthcare services at border sites and in settlement (Rivillas-García et al 2021).

During displacement women and girls face new situations of violence and misogyny, protracted poverty, physical harm and emotional instability. Generally, few migrant women, adolescents (trans- or cisgender) have the opportunity to prepare economically before starting their journey due to sudden circumstances of violence, hunger or poverty that force them to flee their place of origin. Consequently, many of them have little in the way of economic resources when they embark on trip. This situation leads women and adolescents to experience precarious situations such as the inability to afford food, not being able to access accommodation and having to sleep on the street, not having access to transportation to get to a health centre, not being able to buy medicine, among others.

Choices that women and adolescents are forced to make to respond to, and to cope with, such situations faced during displacement are liable to bring about new risks to their health, wellbeing and dignity more broadly. Women may migrate in the hope of finding better jobs, seeking health services, and/or supporting family left behind; yet legal status and the barriers associated with it may constrain choices bringing about a perverse cycle of decisions and risks as coping mechanisms. For instance, women may be (or feel) forced to exchange sex for food, protection, or transport while in displacement (Angulo-Pasel 2018). Of course, 'survival sex' and forced sex might be seen as a false distinction for many women and girls in situations of constraint. In the field of political economy and development, scholars have also explored gendered health vulnerabilities and inequalities as a consequence of exploitation in the labour market or in the informal economy through unpaid/underpaid care work being denied of protection rights and subjects to discriminatory practices and of anti-migrant sentiments (Delgado Wise et al 2013; Bastia 2013; Bastia and Piper 2019).

The outbreak of COVID-19 not only reinforced the needs and harms that made women and girls flee their countries in the first place, but also increased risks as the decision to close borders with Venezuela spread across South America from March 2020. The closure of borders by no means deterred necessary fleers from migrating, it rather brought about new experiences of dispossession, harms and indignities. For example, travelling by *trochas*, an irregular form of travelling that requires walking on alternative, non-urbanized paths through jungle and mountains; and using *trocheros* (smugglers), who engage in illegal migrant trafficking, not only make journeys longer and unsafe, but also subject to arbitrary pronouncements of the smugglers who often demand more payment as they go along, sometimes in the form of (coerced) sexual relations.

This became more problematic during 2020 as many Latin American governments introduced restrictive human mobility measures to reduce the impact of the pandemic. For example, Argentina, Bolivia, Paraguay, Ecuador, Peru and Colombia decreed mandatory quarantine. Ecuador and Peru introduced curfews and like Chile and El Salvador declared a state of emergency, leaving internal security and the custody of health services in the hands of the Armed Forces. Mexico suspended new migrants from accessing shelters and increased border controls and deportations. While these measures attempted to curb the spread of the virus, they also undermined social protection of necessary fleers and exacerbated anti-migration policies and attitudes causing a cycle of even greater risk for displaced populations. In some cases, the economic consequences of lockdown and the inhospitable climate for necessary fleers effectively coerced hundreds of Venezuelan and Central American refugees and migrants to go back along the same route they took to escape and to return to the dangerous, deprived, violent conditions that they were trying to escape in the first place (Riggirozzi et al 2020).

Despite closing borders and generally despite legal restrictions, migration does not stop. If anything, restrictions lead migrants to use informal routes, increasing their vulnerability to exploitation and other harms. Irregular routes and entry points are often controlled by illegal armed groups or criminal organizations, and are real hotspots for (forced) recruitment into sex and human trafficking networks.

This brings to the fore a central claim: the method of travel determines risks and vulnerability to serious violations of fundamental rights. These violations have a differentiated effect on women and girls, because they frequently include sexual assault, have immediate consequences on health and dignity, and deepen long-term gender gaps by trapping women in situations of poverty, violence, including sexual violence, trafficking and exploitation. As one migrant recalled:

> 'We did not have money as such, however, we had some things of value, such as cell phones, our phones; which we had to give the truck driver. We had other things like a hairdryer, a hair straightener … and shoes … and so we paid, to be able to get there.' (Silvia, Manaus, 7 May 2021)

Dispossession, reprioritization and pragmatism are common themes across Venezuelan migrant women and girls. A 15-year-old migrant who crossed by *trocha* to Brazil said: "I prepared all my clothes but in the end lots of that I had to throw on the way because it was heavy and the *trocha* was very muddy, we couldn't carry on the bags" (Liz, Manaus, 18 June 2021). When asked her what advice she would give to other teenagers about to flee Venezuela to Brazil, Liz said: "Just don't bring clothes. I know you love changing clothes, but please, just a bring one piece. Here they give you clothes. And take care of yourself, take care of yourself."

In the majority of the cases, the sense of responsibility towards their children and families is a fundamental factor explaining women's choices to migrate as well as why and how they cope with violence during displacement. Women know that "risks are taken, migrants are exposed to all sorts of things", as expressed by a young Venezuelan migrant: "One of the most difficult things of being a migrant and being a woman is that migrant women are exposed to everything, what one has to face is not easy, even more difficult if that woman is migrating alone" (Gabriela, Manaus, 8 June 2021). As Flavia remarked "migrant women are likely to suffer sexual aggressions" (Flavia, Manaus, 7 May 2021).

Displaced women and girls' experiences are often compounded by situations of coercion, extorsion and sexual violence. Referring to fleers travelling by *trocha* to Colombia, Mayra, who arrived from Venezuela in Cúcuta, Colombia, recalled that in the *trocha*, "there was a pretty girl … a man [smuggler] put his hand on her and told her that if she didn't give him I think it was 10 dollars at that time, they would sexually abused her … there are people like that in the trail" (Bogotá, 12 August 2021).

In many cases women become the main shock absorbers within their families. One 25-year-old interviewee who travelled irregularly to Brazil described it thus:

> 'We had a bad experience at the end of the whole route of the *trocha*, because there were some rogues that subjected us … they wanted us to pay more, although we had paid before … but they wanted me to pay … [and demanded] that I slept with them, and so, well, that

> was a bad experience … I was first angry at my husband because he didn't do anything … but in all conscience, how was he going to do something if they could kill him, he couldn't do anything.' (Flavia, Manaus, 7 May 2021)

The time of the migratory journey also depends on the modality of travel and route taken. In a survey conducted in 2021 with over 1,500 migrant women and adolescent girls from Venezuela crossing to Brazil between 2018 and 2021, Do Carmo Leal et al (2022) report that 83.1 per cent arrived in Brazil within seven days after leaving their homes in Venezuela. Those travelling by bus tend to experience shorter times, up to three days, and enter Brazil using regular pathways, or what a migrant interviewee called '*la Puerta Grande*' (the big gate, to allude to the official crossing point), travelling the southward route towards the 'official' crossing along the border with Brazil, as opposed to by *trochas*, or irregular pathways.

As explained by Sara, a 22-year-old Venezuelan migrant who travelled by trocha with a baby and entered Brazil on 25 December 2020:

> 'To pass the trail it took about two hours walking, then two hours more to arrive at a village where indigenous people gave me something to eat, where to wash and to change clothes, because I had a bag, and in my bag I had everything, but I had to get rid of it, because of the weight, I threw away most of my clothes and my daughter's clothes, I kept the water, my daughter's snacks and papers, the other clothes I threw them down the trail.' (Manaus, 21 June 2021)

Another Venezuelan woman who fled with her two adolescent daughters, aged 14 and 15, explained:

> 'It's horrible. We did not have a drop of water, we had to climb some mountains. We rested a little then we went

> down, almost 6 in the afternoon, it was already dark. … We laid on the ground as we could be seen from the highway, hoping for a Brazilian police car not to pass. Because if they got us, we were going to be deported. We were going to lose the sacrifice of the journey, and of the money spent. We hit the road at midnight. We walked a long way, scared … one of my girls slipped and she grabbed to a branch because she was falling to the void.' (Olga, Manaus, 8 June 2021)

These situations take us to a second claim: most Venezuelan migrants arriving in Brazil and Colombia are impoverished and in need of multiple social and health services. But as they arrive there are a series of legal limitations and barriers as well as situations of rejection and acts of xenophobia on the part of native populations that affect the attainment of the right to health and dignity.

One characteristic aspect within South-South corridors of migration is that often displaced and refugee populations meet saturated local service provision and labour markets, uneven development and austerity, particularly in (border) areas. Furthermore, migrants often experience a higher burden of communicable diseases, chronic diseases, injuries and harms, and mental illness due to conditions at the time of and during the process of displacement, requiring the provision of emergency health and targeted health programmes that are not always available or accessible to them. This is often compounded in settlement countries by fears of foreigners competing for (insufficient) resources causing anti-migrant sentiments.

Colombia's public health system provides emergency services to Venezuelans without documentation. Hospitals along the border report a major spike in emergency room visits by Venezuelans, and Colombian port-of-entry authorities have put in place programmes to vaccinate adults and children out of a concern for highly contagious illnesses like measles, tuberculosis and diphtheria. However, the lack of universal healthcare means that follow-up visits, preventative and chronic health needs, and prescription medicines are simply not available to undocumented migrants. In addition, forced migrants, particularly poor migrants, are usually stigmatized regardless of their legal status and often afraid of seeking care through the formal health systems. Many interviewees settled in Bogotá claimed that they do not seek medical help in hospitals or health centres because they do not have access, particularly if they do not have the appropriate documents; instead they go to the pharmacy because it is easier and more affordable (also Rivillas et al 2018).

Furthermore, although there has been a trend towards regularization – understood as a process through which someone can obtain a residence permit to stay in the country they already live in – since 2021, this was not preceded by a fair and inclusive system of welcome and protection. In August 2017, a year after the massive flux of displaced Venezuelans were becoming a 'crisis' according to Colombian officials, the Colombian government started issuing the Special Temporary Stay Permit (PEP).[1] This was offered to Venezuelan migrants who had entry with passports before July of that year (see Chapter 3). But this excluded Venezuelan nationals whose right to leave the country was curtailed due to passports not being issued in Venezuela. This was something that many women highlighted as leading to mistreatment of women at border checkpoints and other places of control, both in Colombia and in Brazil; the latter, despite seemingly being open to migrants with no passports (at least pre-pandemic), still applied a discretionary policy. As an illustration of how profoundly embedded gendered practices are at the border, one interviewee recalls the Brazilian authorities' lack of respect for her, as a mother responsible for four children:

> 'It was all very bad because I have my passport, my eldest daughter too, but for the other two I couldn't get them, it was difficult to get them in Venezuela. In Pacaraima, it was very hard, because the military told me to "take them

> back to their country", because they would not allow the children to cross "illegally", or without documents, to Brazil, as they said. … The military wouldn't let us enter, and I had to spend all night trying to find a way in, because I couldn't turn back. … He [an Army officer] said, "if I let you in, your children would come in illegally and this would unresponsible on your part … go back to your country … you can't come to Brazil" … I cried and then, thank God, one of the taxis came and we could hide our children inside it to enter Brazil illegally.' (Mirza, Manaus, 30 June 2021)

While Colombia and Brazil remain major destinations for Venezuelans fleeing the crisis, these rules – combined with major obstacles to obtaining documents in their home country – placed thousands of Venezuelans at risk of legal irregularity which deepens risks of exploitation, work restricted to the informal sector, and further abuse. As explored in Chapter 3, Colombia is quite new as a refugee/migrant hosting state and has limited the grounds for granting citizenship to children born to immigrants with irregular status, while Venezuela's crisis prevents its citizens from readily obtaining documentation. The result is a normative framework that prevents many from benefiting from social programmes, including access to healthcare, restricts mobility rights, and, in many cases, locks them out of participation in the formal economy and other social and political spaces.

By the beginning of 2021, when approximately 2 million of the over 5 million Venezuelans who fled the country were based in Colombia, the government made some efforts to include Venezuelans in their pandemic response (Cubillos-Novella et al 2020). However, the health crisis and COVID-19 related measures, such as quarantine, meant that (with almost half of Venezuelan migrants in Colombia dependent on work in the informal sector; Bahar et al 2020), they faced poverty and forced evictions, despite OHCHR's recommendations that these be prohibited during the COVID-19 outbreak (OHCHR 2020). Without financial support or access to public funds, and unable to earn a living, many faced becoming homeless and destitute in a foreign country and had no alternative but to return to Venezuela, either by bus, if they could afford it, or on foot. Their return of course put them and their families at risk. Without the income that migrants earn working abroad, migrants' families faced not only hunger, but also harassment by nationals, as well as lack of access to healthcare, extending and deepening the crisis of livelihoods and conflict that gives rise to the necessity of migration and displacement in the first place.

As COVID-19 related border restrictions ease, fleers still must navigate a complicated bureaucratic system to obtain residence permits and gain access to Colombia's state services. Until then, they are not allowed to use official buses at the border to take them to other destinations or transit points, shelter or any sort of support. The result is protracted displacement, unsafe temporary accommodation, often in hotels, further poverty and risks of sexual and labour abuse and of organized crime.

In Brazil, Venezuelans have been recognized as refugees under the Cartagena Declaration, and enjoy social protection entitlements, as detailed in Chapter 3. Furthermore, Brazil's Constitution created a universal public health system (Sistema Único de Saúde, SUS) which, by law, grants free access to healthcare to nationals and non-nationals regardless of migration status (Guerra and Ventura 2017). The Constitution also set out straightforward provisions to safeguard the right to health of women, particularly in relation to sexual and reproductive health (Bustreo and Hunt 2013), although Riggirozzi (2021) draws attention to the daily experience of gender-based social relations and tensions reflecting social, political and health divisions, and economic stressors that prevent many women, particularly from ethnic minorities, from exercising their rights to (health) equality.

Despite seemingly 'progressive' migration and refugee laws, a number of vetoes and arbitrary decisions by former President Michel Temer and his successor Jair Bolsonaro (2019–2022) limited the scope and reach of the refugee laws in favour of ad hoc temporary permits for Venezuelan displaced persons in the country (Fernandes and Jubilut 2018; Vera Espinoza et al 2021). Furthermore, increasing levels of violence and xenophobia have meant that displaced Venezuelans face many barriers to accessing services and, more fundamentally, integrating into the 'host' society.

As noted earlier, governing migration is not just challenging because of numbers arriving at border area towns, but also because these localities often already have their own socioeconomic struggles. For example, the majority of Venezuelans have been arriving at the northern state of Roraima, the smallest and poorest state in Brazil. The main crossing point is a small Brazilian town called Pacaraima, at the very northern-most tip of the country, and Boa Vista is the capital of the state. While Pacaraima has received around 1,000 migrants a day in 2019, Boa Vista has become home to 40 per cent of the Venezuelans who have taken refuge in Brazil, increasing its population of 340,000 by 60,000 in the three years since 2015 (Surita 2020). The upsurge in the number of displaced people at the border put enormous pressure on local public services, which became overloaded, particularly the health sector, given the poor health suffered by many displaced Venezuelans. For example, according to data from the Ministry of Health in Brazil, in Boa Vista, there is only one maternity hospital. It saw an increase of births among Venezuelan migrants from 3.4 per cent of all deliveries in Boa Vista in 2016 to 26.1 per cent in 2019 (DataSUS 2020; Bahamondes et al 2020). As noted in Chapter 3, as a way of containment and response, in 2018, the government of Brazil set up Operation Welcome (*Operação Acolhida*), a federal inter-agency operation involving the Armed Forces, government services and international organizations such as

UNHCR and IOM, to manage the unprecedented flows of Venezuelans at the main point of entry in Roraima. Operation Welcome meant that people arriving in Roraima could get in line to request refugee status, request residency permits, get vaccinations and be allocated to an official shelter. In this context, Operation Welcome was implemented to offer both humanitarian support, and provide order and control through shelter, food, and access to health services (Moulin and Magalhães 2020). Yet the increasing numbers also challenged sheltering capacity. UNICEF (2021) estimated that over 2,000 migrants – of a total of 19,000 people that live in Pacaraima – were living in the streets while waiting for documentation, a situation unseen since the most acute moments of the Venezuelan migration outflow in 2017 and 2018, and that multiplied 15 times between June and August 2021, after the reopening of the borders closed since March 2020.

With local services strained and labour markets in Roraima unable to easily absorb new arrivals, tensions increased, sometimes leading to outbreaks of violence (Moulin and Magalhães 2020). In August 2018, for example, hundreds of local residents gathered around homeless Venezuelans camping on the streets, taunting its inhabitants and burning people's belongings (La Opinion 2018). On some occasions, violence was exercised by the same institutions that were allegedly there to protect, such as the Federal Police. It entered independent shelters managed by religious organizations, such as *Pastoral do Migrante*, in search of 'undocumented' migrants to deport. The manager of a shelter that gives refuge only to Venezuelan migrant women and children said that the "police enter armed and with no court order authorising that type of action" (also Fernandes and Oliveira 2021).

Other examples of violence faced by women and girls relate to intimate-partner violence and violence in shelters, where many women expressed feeling insecure. One interviewee recalled the 'feminicide' of a woman she met in a shelter, who had no family connections or social network in Brazil. Fractured social networks can further impact displaced women's safety. For example, one participant mentioned the physical violence she suffered from her partner for six years, while feeling unable to leave him because she "do[es] not have anybody here in Brazil" (Flavia, Manaus, 7 May 2021).

As explored by Wolf (2020) in her analysis of Venezuelan women in Colombia, hyper sexualization, harassment, sexual abuse and exploitation commonly violate female migrants' rights, which are entrenched in lingering conservatism and patriarchal attitudes towards women, sexuality, and family roles in Latin America. These attitudes create barriers to the integration of migrants in new societies, and limit how the duty of states and state agencies to protect women and girls is understood and operationalized (also Riggirozzi 2020).

Barriers and determinants of sexual and reproductive health (and rights) in displacement

As discussed in Chapters 1 and 3, international frameworks have been important in putting migrants' right to health on the global agenda. States have a duty to respect and guarantee the right to health without discrimination to everyone within their borders. Restricting access to healthcare to populations because of their legal status is a violation of international human rights norms. Yet, as Hennebry and Petrozziello (2019: 124–9) argue, 'states fall short of proposals that guarantee migrants' and refugees' access to gender-responsive healthcare services … especially in relation to reproductive and sexual health care, pre- and post-natal care, services for sexually transmitted infections and specialized care for sexual violence survivors'. Hence while the health of migrants, particularly women and girls, has been mainstreamed in international frameworks, there are still lags and gaps in terms of operationalizing the language around migrant and gender-responsiveness systems of protection at national levels to enable the realization of rights, freedoms and dignity of all migrants, particularly of displaced women and girls. From this perspective, and based on the case of Venezuelan displaced women and girls, we identify lags and gaps in protection that act as barriers to the satisfaction of health needs and rights, particularly those regarding to sexual and reproductive health, and to achieving (global and national) health and equity.

The first barrier relates to the conditions of the journey and the challenges faced by women and girls on the move and at arrival in places of abode. The mass migration of Venezuelans, increasingly made up of women, young pregnant mothers and mothers with infants or young children, face difficult journeys compounded by risks of sexual violence, malnutrition, hunger and thirst, particularly for those who travel by irregular pathways "who often are left traumatised" (Jovana, Manaus, 10 June 2021).

Borders and border control are also determinants of gendered health risks and rights satisfaction. The way migrant women and girls arrive determines who or which institution receives them (if at all), what information and guidance they receive, whether the documentation they need to access shelter and the health system is explained to them. Their legal status may further influence their opportunities to enjoy the right to health and live their life with dignity. Border towns are critical spaces that can offer opportunities for inclusion or create gaps in terms of information on documentation to access shelters and the universal health system. If migrants do not enter through the official entry gate, they are likely to miss out on available information on shelters, healthcare facilities and rights. Consequently, if migrant women and girls become invisible to systems of protection in place, they fall into the cracks of such systems and most probably end up relying on illegal networks of exploitation and control, and face a new scale of gender risks, harms, abusive relationships, and an unending spiral of rights denial.

A second barrier to the upholding of rights and the right to health relates to time. Time on the street waiting to be sheltered, to receive information and documentation, to be regularized, to find a job, waiting for access to medical care, time on the street during the day because migrants must leave night shelters, and so on. These are all interrelated and gendered factors that create situations of risk, powerlessness and indignity for migrant women and girls (Roth 2021). This is even more problematic for those who enter the country through irregular routes because they are more likely to be undocumented and thus invisible to the system. Information is mostly accessible and delivered through official operations, as well as in shelters.

There is a third barrier that is more structural and relates to conditions in shelters. Shelters, like those operated by the Brazilian Armed Forces, or emergency hotel accommodation provided in Colombia can mitigate some of the immediate needs experienced by Venezuelans by providing food, temporary housing and information on accessing health services. However, there are a variety of structural gender vulnerabilities linked to dangerous, under-resourced and overcrowded accommodation facilities that create and reproduce situations of indignity and damage to the health of migrant women and girls.

Some reported cases of "urinary tract infections due to the conditions of the bathrooms", lack of privacy and security, and general discomfort from sleeping on "thin mats on the floor", particularly in the shelters built at the Manaus bus terminal, which operate only during the night. Lack of privacy is an issue for adolescent girls who may feel uncomfortable changing sanitary pads during menstruation in communal toilets, particularly as they are encouraged to use and clean menstrual cups, often provided by international organizations. As reported by UNFPA (2018), the lack of shelter, or overcrowded and under-resourced shelters and camps, where women have to share scarcely illuminated bathrooms, increase the risk of gender violence, including sexual violence. Many of our interviewees find that shelters and temporary accommodation in hotels do not provide an environment where they can live a life free from violence, particularly in night shelters that are set up only for sleeping in bus stations, and especially for transgender migrants. For example, Ingrid, a trans women interviewed in Manaus, recalled:

> 'It was not easy here in Brazil since I arrived. First I was rough sleeping then I went to a night shelter. I suffered a bit, was abused, they [alluding to men in the shelter] cut my hair by force and sexually abused me. It has not been easy indeed.' (5 July 2021)

Poverty is another barrier to the enjoyment of the right to health. Migrant women and girls acting as sole caregivers often must prioritize the health and wellbeing of their children or those under their care over their own. In particular, the health risks of exhaustion and of becoming trapped in the cycle of poverty are increased by the caregiving conditions experienced by migrant women. Providing care is closely linked to access to decent work. Many women expressed their inability to access decent and formal jobs, since they could not find someone to take care of their children while they worked. Because of this, they were either unable to work or took their children with them to informal workplaces. Socioeconomic conditions directly influence the experience of integration and wellbeing of migrants and thus their health.

There is also the risk that migrant women living in poverty will be sexually exploited, given the urgent needs, such as hunger and homelessness, that they and their families face. Rape and sexual exploitation increase the exposure to health and security risks such as unwanted pregnancies, unsafe abortions, sexually transmitted diseases, as well as human trafficking and other forms of violence. Specific policies are needed to improve migrant women's access to formal employment, alongside policies that effectively enforce the law against rape and sexual exploitation of migrant women and adolescents. Otherwise, there is a risk of prolonged poverty for women in the migrant community through cycles of casual, informal or exploitative relationships, including those of work and unemployment.

Many interviewees expressed that language affected their ability to adequately search, communicate and engage with health services. The reality of language barriers is an additional impediment to the ability to seek and access appropriate healthcare and, in some cases, is an example of institutional and interpersonal discrimination. This is particularly difficult for victims of violence who may not be able to access health and support services or, if they do, may feel uncomfortable having to disclose situations of indignity to authorities or health professionals through a translator.

Finally, as explored in Chapter 3, different legal frameworks will determine who is entitled to healthcare in displacement. There are legal determinants of health that could act as barriers to the provision of the right to health of forcibly displaced women and girls, their health outcomes and equity. We use the term legal determinants of health because, as Gostin et al (2019) propose, it demonstrates the power of legal and normative frameworks to both structure practices in and across societies regarding treatment and entitlement of migrants, and to redress underlying social and economic causes of physical and psychological harm and disease for whom necessary health protection standards in transit and countries of abode become reduced to a legal status.

Hence, we propose that a forced migration–health–gender nexus is defined by a set of challenges that women and girls face throughout the cycle of displacement and that relates to deprivations, trauma and violence as well as challenges around accessing public healthcare along the journey and in places of abode. We identify the nexus in Figure 4.1.

Many health risks and needs are exacerbated on arrival and settlement as displaced women and girls encounter

Figure 4.1: Sexual and reproductive health risks and needs in and because of displacement

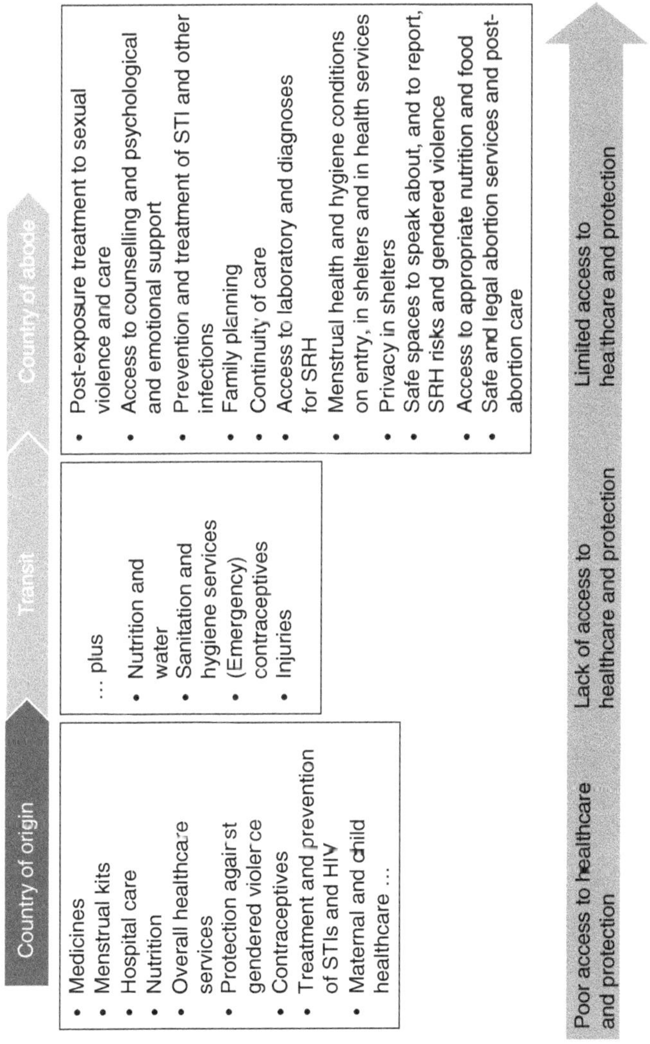

many barriers to the access of healthcare and the enjoyment of the right to health, all of which inhibit the ability of displaced women and girls to integrate in new societies and to develop healthy, autonomous and dignified lives. In our assessment many of the SRH needs during and because of displacement become unmet needs due to barriers that affect the enjoyment of health rights of migrants, and the SRH of migrant women and girls in particular. The barriers and the consequences of those barriers not only are determinants of unmet health needs, but also create conditions that reproduce further (sexual and reproductive) health vulnerabilities and risks. This is summarized in Figure 4.2 where we also identify how consequences of barriers cause serious harm, creating, intentionally or not, obstacles to the achievement of the human rights of migrants, including the right to health.

The assessment of gendered risks, SRH needs, barriers to accessing healthcare and protection of women and girls in displacement in the context of migration laws and governance in previous chapters suggests that there are at least four likely scenarios affecting the exercise of the right to health (and other rights) that if not addressed would reproduce gendered inequalities for the forcibly displaced, as seen on Table 4.1.

Building on the above, we present one more claim: poor and unmet health needs and rights, particularly those relating to SRH, further entrench disadvantage and inequities for displaced women and girls, inhibiting their potential for living healthy and safe lives, and engaging in autonomous choices with respect to their immediate social and economic environment as well as their future.

Who should protect? Whose responsibility it is to protect women and girls in displacement, particularly those who had to flee their country of origin and that arrive with needs that have arisen because of their displacement? How should we think about what displaced women and girls are entitled to in terms of the protection and safeguarding of their human right to health?

Figure 4.2: Barriers to accessing sexual and reproductive health services and rights

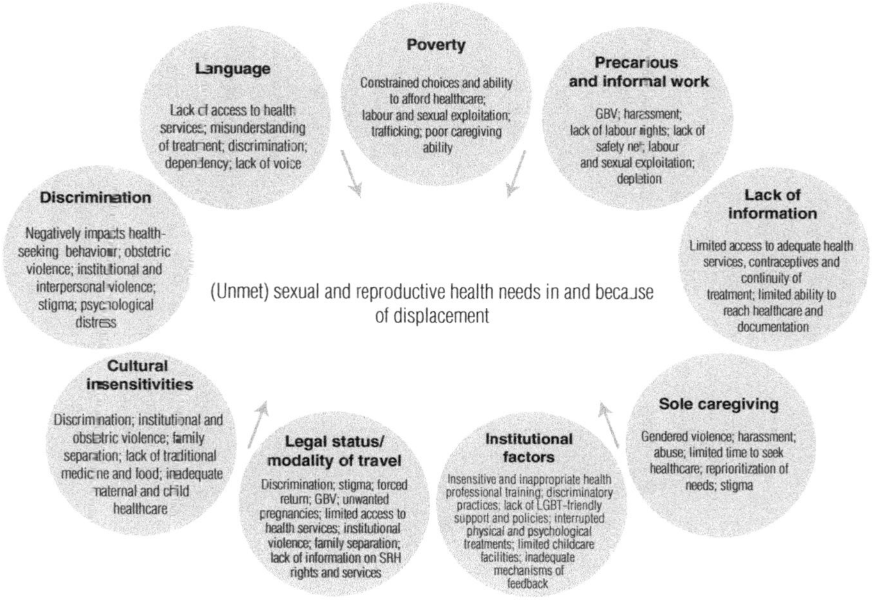

Source: Riggirozzi et al (2023)

Table 4.1: Key scenarios underpinning the sexual and reproductive health inequality of female fleers

Key scenarios underpinning (SRH) inequality	Quotes from female fleers
1. Lacking right to (non-emergency) healthcare	"Because we are migrants, I feel that we have less rights to access certain services, because we don't have proper papers … I also feel that when you don't know what you're entitled to, it's easier to be afraid and not seek healthcare. I don't know if the hospital is going to deport me or if I'm going to end up getting into trouble. … Sometimes they [providers] tell us that they won't see us because we do not have the right documents." (Ana, Bogotá, 19 August 2021)
	"Two or three weeks ago a Venezuelan girl I know had pain in her kidneys, a horrible pain … and she went to the hospital twice and was not treated, so I told her to go to the chemist, but she needed to pay for the treatment. That's when the girl started to improve. … Here not having the papers in order, having nothing, take away migrants' chances of being treated in healthcare services." (Nancy, Bogotá, 12 August 2021)
	"Honestly, yes, I think migrants refrain from seeking healthcare when they are irregular because, I mean, they are very afraid, do you understand me? That's why, because we are immigrants, there is always rejection, always … all Venezuelans have suffered a rejection." (Carla, Bogotá, 19 August 2021)
2. Having formal rights, but lacking documents and/or resources to access healthcare	"They also said I needed to bring a document [that I didn't have] so that the gynaecologist could see me or to have a scan made or something like that. They would tell me to come back at a certain time, I would, and in the end I'd never get the appointment." (Maria, Manaus, 23 May 2021)
	"The biggest challenge is documentation. There is a rule that if you don't have your documents, you have nothing, and nobody will see you. Only with the health card can you be seen to. So this is one of the first challenges for migrants in Brazil." (Jesica, Manaus, 9 June 2021)
	"I have some issues in my legs, but I have never been able to set an appointment because they always refused me. I don't understand. It seems I have to show them something. I have brought the tests I did in Venezuela, but they don't seem to have any value here." (Bruna, Manaus, 22 June 2021)

Table 4.1: Key scenarios underpinning the sexual and reproductive health inequality of female fleers (continued)

Key scenarios underpinning (SRH) inequality	Quotes from female fleers
	"As a woman alone … one feels very vulnerable … in terms of protection or health support, there is no support unless you're dying. If you don't have money to buy painkillers you will feel pain, because they won't provide you with one in shelters." (Patricia, Manaus, 4 June 2021) "I walked a lot to find out where the nearest health service was, I walked almost two hours with my son in my arms, to get to the health post. There, I arrived and presented my identity card and birth certificate, and they gave me my health card and my son's. I didn't have money to pay for transport to go." (Eliane, Manaus, 24 June 2021) "The first time I went to the health services, I didn't have my health card so they dismissed me … they told me 'no, we can't help you without the health card'. So they requested the card for me. The card arrived about a month later, because everything there was slow, but at least it arrived." (Mirza, Manaus, 30 June 2021)
3. Having formal rights and partial ability to access healthcare but confronting cultural and language barriers	"Language, language is an impediment to everything, well, because you want to express your pain, you want to express what you feel, and many times people don't understand, then you get frustrated … language and not having the financial resources are the greatest barriers." (Patricia, Manaus, 4 June 2021) "Some Venezuelans tell me that they are treated badly in the health units because they don't speak Portuguese … and that's why Brazilians do whatever they want with Venezuelans." (Marcia, Manaus, 10 June 2021) "Because of the language most of them [health service providers] don't make you feel comfortable saying much to them. Thank God that I already know how to express myself better, at first it was worse." (Bruna, Manaus, 22 June 2021) "Some health service providers may not be patient … being a Venezuelan they treat one in a derogatory manner, they do not have the patience to explain to us, they are not interested in learning the Spanish language, we are forced to learn Portuguese." (Luisa, Manaus, 29 June 2021)

(continued)

Table 4.1: Key scenarios underpinning the sexual and reproductive health inequality of female fleers (continued)

Key scenarios underpinning (SRH) inequality	Quotes from female fleers
4. Having formal rights plus at least partial ability to access healthcare but confronting disrespectfulness, misogyny, patronizing professional attitudes	"Because in Boa Vista the health system was not helping me, ignoring me rather, I had to move on, to be able to achieve what I was looking for, which is my operation." (Marcela, Manaus, 8 June 2021) "Honestly, I don't like going to the doctor's here, because when I do, I ask many health service providers where I should go to, they tell me I should to X place ... when I get there, they send me elsewhere, and again and again. ... In the end I never get the assistance." (Maria, Manaus, 23 May 2021) "...when my belly was giving me severe pain ... then I had to walk and walk because it hurt, it hurt a lot. ... I didn't know what things are like here in Brazil, I was scared. They told me that when you are going to give birth, 'liquid has to come out first', the water has to break so you can give birth. ... Yes, they told me ... 'here it's not like in Venezuela, here it's different, because here in Brazil first the waters have to break to be able to give birth ... so you have to wait'. I didn't know, it hurt around [my waist]. I had to walk, they sent me to walk ... and waited and waited, everything to be able for the waters to break." (Alenia, Manaus, 21 August 2021)

Conclusion

The process of displacement is a determinant of (sexual and reproductive) health of migrant women and, in many cases, such as that of the Venezuelan fleers, women leave precisely because of the failure to fulfil their SRH rights. Our primary focus in this chapter has been on this element of the gendered dimension of the process of movement and settlement for those who are forcibly displaced: the effects on, and challenges to, SRH of displacement.

We approached this issue by analysing the lived experience of women and girls fleers from Venezuela to contextualize how the current international refugee protection systems, built around the migrant–refugee distinction, has been translated into regional and domestic frameworks, and hence expressed in differentiated access to rights in Brazil and in Colombia, with (gendered) effects on displaced women's access to SRH care and protection.

The detailed analysis of SRH risks and challenges faced by women and girls in (and because of) displacement, and the continuum we see from place of origin to that of abode, offers an opportunity to evaluate responses and potential 'protection gaps' that emerge in the ways in which normative frameworks and policies are construed and implemented, affecting responses and the provision of services that are another source of health vulnerability for migrant women. The focus on the lived experience of necessary fleers also places attention on the social protection and care of migrants and the gender inequalities that continue to limit women's and girls' freedoms despite legislative frameworks to address violence against women, progress in women's education, and economic, social and political participation.

Gender-based violence, sexual violence, poverty, insecurities and barriers to the access of services and rights affect women and girls in domestic and public spheres, and are clear consequences of persisting gender inequalities and injustices in migration. Building on these injustices and addressing gendered needs regarding the SRH of women and the responsibilities of states and international agencies to provide protection, this chapter has evaluated the implementation of refugee and migrant statuses in terms of whether they address the protection needs of the female mobile population and their rights relating to SRH.

We exposed how deficient policy dialogues and normative frameworks devoid of gendered rights, language and perspectives limit protection, despite progressive legislation and humanitarian programmes that respond to emergencies but do not redress migration injustices and take shared responsibility to protect people on the move. The consequences, as we have showed, are unmet health needs and overall systems that fail migrant women and girls and (even if unintentionally) create spaces for differential risks to happen in mobility and settlement, all compounded by intersecting inequalities exacerbated by exclusionary policies and institutional responses.

The next chapter picks up from this, investigating the important question of who is responsible for ensuring the protection of the SRH rights of displaced women. In answering the question, it draws out the implications of the reconceptualization of displaced persons as necessary fleers for the distribution of responsibility and the forms of protection owed to them.

FIVE

Responsibility and the Ethics of Forced Displacement in South America

Our empirically grounded socio-legal analysis of the predicaments of displaced Venezuelan women and girls in relation to protection and secure access to SRH rights highlights a range of obstacles to the enjoyment of these rights and more generally of recognition of their dignity. In this chapter, we address the requirements of protection and of the enjoyment of SRH rights, and provide an analysis of the distribution of responsibility for securing such conditions. We begin by returning to the challenges confronted by female necessary fleers in transit, in places of immediate refuge and in settlement, before turning to situate these in the 'necessary fleer' framework and the core principles of protection that it establishes. This is followed by abstract and general reflections on responsibility, contextualized in relation to the Venezuelan displacement. We distinguish the different roles and responsibilities of a range of actors that encompass governmental and non-governmental agents as well as the displaced women and girls themselves. Finally, we locate this account of protection and responsibility within a wider justice and development framework that addresses the conditions that generate necessary flight.

Protection gaps and obstacles to enjoying rights

Given their compelling reasons for flight, Venezuelan women and girls face the initial challenge of passage to the border of a neighbouring state as a place of immediate refuge. Passage is important in two different but related respects. The first is that different forms of passage may involve very different levels of risk, and especially of gendered risks of sexual assault and violence. The second is that the form of entry can significantly affect the legal status assigned to those who flee with effects on their ability to access SRH rights. The relationship between the two is that a destination state's border policies may effectively require some fleers to take irregular routes to border crossing when borders are closed to all (for example, during the pandemic) or to those who have reasonable grounds of flight (for example, because their claims do not fit well with the 1951 Convention or they lack required forms of documentation such as passports). This is one determinant in shaping their (il)legal status once they have crossed the border.

In what became a global pandemic of exclusions with states closing their borders to all comers (against WHO advice) in the face of the spread of the COVID-19 virus, asylum seekers globally were a casualty (Lenard 2020), often with devastating effects. Border closure does not stop movement, it simply increases its danger. In the Venezuelan context, this meant, first, that necessary fleers had to engage in *trocha* journeys, which empowered (and generated conflicts between rival) smuggler gangs seeking control of a lucrative business with the predictable effect (Collins 2021), as the women and girls attest, that sexual exploitation, assault and violence all significantly increased. Second, necessary fleers were often subsequently positioned as irregular undocumented migrants with all the attendant exacerbation of their vulnerability that this practically entailed.

Once the displaced Venezuelan women and girls have reached a state of first refuge, they confront further challenges for their sexual and reproductive health. Some of these, as we have shown, may be the product of migration statuses that work in practice to obstruct their access to, and exercise of, sexual and reproductive rights in form of medical services and to obstruct enjoyment of conditions of reasonable security from exposure to sexual exploitation, assault and violence. Others may be products of generalized conditions such as lack of capacity to protect in the places of temporary abode or unwillingness on the part of municipal, provincial or national government to provide the degree of protection required. There are also more specific issues relating to problems of, for example, insecure accommodation, lack of gender or cultural sensitivity in provision of health services, limited access to official employment (often related to lack of childcare), and local hostility to necessary fleers. In recent reports, xenophobia is spiking against the background of the effects of the pandemic. Amnesty International (2022: 29) highlights the continuing failure in Colombia (and Peru) 'to provide adequate protection for the women, who often face physical and sexual violence at home, but also exploitation at work, including being co-opted into sexual exploitation', noting that in spite 'of high levels of under-reporting, GBV cases rose 71 per cent between 2018 and 2021 in Colombia'.

There is also a consequential risk associated with lack of or inadequate protection that create barriers to integration in society. CARE (2020: 29) reported that integration of Venezuelan migrants and refugees, particularly those (perceived to be) in irregular situations, is limited and slow in Colombia and across other countries in South America. To a large extent this is due to xenophobia that also limits access to basic services, including housing, employment and justice. For women and adolescent girls, this is compounded by high levels of stigma and hypersexualized perception, which leaves them particularly vulnerable to sexual violence and exploitation. Many women interviewed in Colombia told us how they were offered shelter by Colombian men, often in hotels. On many occasions, this led into situations of domestic servitude, including sex slavery. Others encountered harassment or job offers that came with the expectation of sexual favours, and women working in bars and massage parlours are treated as sexual objects. Many others are forced or coerced to engage in transactional or survival sex. CARE (2020) also reported that in Ocaña in Norte de Santander, Colombia, 90 per cent of the sex workers were Venezuelan, and that often they lacked documentation. Many of our interviewees in Brazil and Colombia reported high levels of harassment by men in the street. It was also found that women in precarious employment situations, especially those with irregular status, frequently faced a paradoxical 'choice' between keeping their positions or suffering abuse and harassment. Without jobs, migrant women in Brazil became even more dependent on the humanitarian infrastructure and programmes created for them. Some would go to 'night shelters', overnight sleeping facilities based at bus stations, which interviewees regarded as highly unsafe for women and girls, especially transgender women. One interviewee explained how she was abused near the bus station where she spent nights, making her 'choose' to move to the streets.

Responsibility to protect is not *only* a question of addressing protection in the form of delivering health campaigns or providing shelter, all of which are central to meeting the rights and sexual and reproductive health needs as explored in the previous chapter. It *also* points to the fundamental need to redress underlying social issues such as sexualization and stigma in ways that can support sustainable agency and integration of displaced women and girls.

Necessary fleers and principles of protection

Our motivation for adopting the 'necessary fleer' framework is grounded in a crucial feature exemplified by the flight of Venezuelans and the responses to that flight by destination states. This is the danger of making protection conditional on specific reasons for flight or modes of entry. While it may be the case, as Owen (2020) argues (and Aleinikoff and Zamore 2019, acknowledge), that different types of necessary fleers may be entitled to varied types of protective response (thus, for example, those actively persecuted by their governments may require new state membership more immediately than those fleeing breakdown of public order), the form of protection that we are concerned with in this study refers to the general protection that should be available to all those who have practically necessitating reasons for flight and require protection of important human rights (such as the right to sexual and reproductive health). Access to such protection should not depend on the mode of entry into the state of first refuge. In other words, the concept of necessary fleer disables the migrant–refugee binary effects we traced in Chapter 2 in terms of instituting arbitrary hierarchies of differential access to rights that are more geared towards the interest of states in controlling displaced populations than to the dignity of those displaced. This is important because the different migration statuses assigned to female necessary fleers were not simply a function of the form of their entry but also (in the context of the evolving responses of Brazil, Colombia and other South American states to mass Venezuelan displacement) of the timing of their entry, of their possession of (or access to) various forms of documentation, and of the political interests of the government in the receiving state. Under the ethical framework of necessary flight, by contrast, the recognition by South American states that conditions in Venezuela amounted to a situation of 'serious and generalized violation of human rights' would establish a group-based criterion of access of international protection that would cover each and every Venezuelan seeking refuge whenever and however they come to be in a state of immediate refuge. In certain respects, we might see the introduction of the PEP in Colombia in 2021 as a partial step towards this position, although Venezuelan women face a number of challenges in obtaining a PEP. As stated by Amnesty International (2022: 22):

> The first is associated with the presenting evidence. Given that many have entered without passing through an official border crossing, live in precarious conditions, are unable to enrol their children in the education system, and only approach health services for emergencies, it is not possible for them to present a document proving that they entered the country before 31 January 2021.

As we have seen, for contingent political reasons, Brazil too has come, partially and imperfectly, to acknowledge the general claim to protection of Venezuelans fleers.

This ethical framework also highlights the point that the concept of necessary fleer as a practical category for organizing responses to contexts of mass displacement stresses the strict duty on states to maintain the openness of the border to those who have reasons of practical necessity for their flight. This is particularly important in contexts such as the COVID-19 pandemic where border closures had the effect of undermining the opportunity for (relatively) safe passage. This point expresses the first principle of protection of the necessary fleer framework:

Safety: *a right to access a safe place and not to be returned to danger.* The former encompasses a duty of safe passage so that the costs of exercising the right to access a safe place are not unreasonable, while the latter should acknowledge not only the conditions of the displaced person's home state but also whether it is reasonable to ask them to leave the new life they have made (Aleinikoff and Zamore 2019: 56–68).

The principle of safety is the first principle because it expresses the condition under which the following four principles of protection become operative. We can understand these as establishing the fundamental orientation to being able to live with dignity. Recall the distinction that we drew from

Rosen (2012) between 'respect as observance' and 'respect as respectfulness'. The former addresses the dignity *of* one's person as a bearer of equal status expressed in terms of human rights; the latter acknowledges the dignity *in* one's person that grounds one's entitlement to equal status. We can see the four further principles of protection as seeking to secure these two dimensions of dignity:

Rebuilding lives and communities: Where there is no immediately foreseeable prospect of safe return, displaced persons 'must be given the opportunity to rebuild their lives and to reconstitute communities in which individual lives take shape and derive meaning' (Aleinikoff and Zamore 2019: 69). As Owen (2020) argues, the forcibly displaced are characterized by the loss of effective citizenship –the loss of reasonable conditions of effective social agency for which operative citizenship should play protective and enabling functions. Added to the social powerlessness in the home state and typically also in transit is the social disorientation that comes with arrival in the unfamiliar social environment of another state. To repair this situation means providing safe passage to those in transit and to provide displaced persons with conditions under which they can reasonably experience themselves as effective social agents. They can then make choices and plans about their futures that are not simply driven by the urgent requirements of practical necessity and have some ability to shape the social environment in which those choices and plans are made (Owen 2020). As Aleinikoff and Zamore (2019: 75) note, in practice this entails 'that displacement constitutes a development challenge and that development aid is a crucial component of any comprehensive response', but we may add that insofar as displaced persons are able to rebuild their lives, they can also act as agents of development when appropriately enabled to do so.

Solutions: 'An effective system of international protection should seek as quickly as possible to end displacement and the need for international protection' (Aleinikoff and Zamore

2019: 76). Aleinikoff and Zamore interpret the concept of solution as referring to a situation in which '[1951] Convention rights and other applicable international human rights norms are being fully respected by hosting states, including the principle of non-return (so that there will be no return to danger), when economic, social and political conditions in hosting states are conducive to human flourishing, and when displaced persons have some kind of right to remain in states that are hosting them' (Aleinikoff and Zamore 2019: 78).

Mobility: 'Persons should be able to seek protection, travel within states of asylum, and be provided opportunities to move to other regime members' (Aleinikoff and Zamore 2019: 85). The provision of travel identification documents and the presumptive right of displaced persons to have opportunities to move between different states participating in the regime of international protection requires contextual working out, but we agree with Aleinikoff and Zamore that mobility as a part of respect for the agency of displaced persons is a matter of significance both within states and across states that, especially in regional contexts, states should aim to cooperate to achieve.

Voice: Necessary fleers should enjoy voice in relation to the regime of protection to which they are subject at scales ranging from the local to the global; the core democratic principle is that those subject to rule should have a say in the rule to which they are subject, whether takes the forms of democratizing refugee camps or integrating refugee voices into municipal government into contexts of locality-based protection or many other possible forms (Aleinikoff and Zamore 2019: 85–7). Access to voice – to being listened to and having one's reasons count in deliberative contexts concerning the rules to which one is subject – is a central part of what we have referred to as 'respect as respectfulness'.

The specific focus of our project is on displaced women and SRH rights, so it is pertinent to reflect on the principles of protection in relations to SRH rights of necessary fleers:

- *Safety*: Security of SRH rights in the context of safe passage, of safe resting points and safe places of first refuge is a central part of what 'safety' means for women and girls, and poses challenges of resourcing (for example, access to sanitary towels and medical care), of organization (such as women migrant's collective action for self-care), and of protection (for example, preventing sexual assault and exploitation). The demands of securing safety involve different challenges at different points of the journey of displacement that engage with a range of other private and public actors who may hinder or help in securing safety. Safety of SRH rights is not just a constituent of safety overall but is also dependent on it; the decision to accept sexual exploitation in return for the protection of a male migrant, for example, indicates how a lack of access to safe passage undermines access to secure SRH rights. This also matters for the organization of temporary sites of protection for displaced persons in the receiving state as, for example, temporary shelters such as the ones found at the bus station in Boa Vista, Brazil, where beds are located side by side under tents in an open plan, with no privacy whatsoever, may leave women and girls highly exposed to sexual assault.
- *Rebuilding lives and communities*: Enjoyment of SRH is part of a flourishing life and hence being able to exercise SRH rights is a core part of enjoying effective social agency for women and girls, but enjoyment of SRH is also tied in important ways to access to welfare, education and employment, and participation rights in the local community as sites where women and girls can meet each other and potential partners (male, female or other) as well as articulate and address common concerns. Building links with non-displaced women and girls in places of temporary or permanent settlement through women's group or via NGOs concerned with women's issues or in other ways is an integral part of meeting long-term responsibilities to address trauma and cultivating confidence in reporting

sexual violence as well as securing SRH as a constituent element of a flourishing life in community with others.

- *Solutions*: Secure SRH rights are integral to conditions of a dignified life in the hosting states.
- *Mobility*: Both intra-state movement and opportunities for inter-state movement are important in relation to SRH rights contexts. Enabling women and girls to leave when these are negative contexts of abuse or exploitation or when movement for reasons – employment or education, among others – that enhance the agency of women and girls offers positive outcomes for their ability to access and exercise SRH rights. Self-directed mobility can serve both protective and enabling functions with respect to SRH rights.
- *Voice*: This is a critical issue for SRH rights because it is central to the ability of women and girls to develop collective consciousness of their rights as well as to inform and hold to account government agencies, NGOs and health service providers with respect to SRH rights and to call and organize for reforms in international, regional, national and local policies in their practice.

Addressing SRH rights cannot therefore be separated out from the overall principles of protection and their wider implementation – but how that implementation is conducted will be highly context-dependent and needs to be responsive to existing laws, norms, material circumstances and actors in the specific contexts of forced displacement being addressed. One theme that the importance of voice highlights is that working out such context-dependent implementation of the more general norms must be a process that includes women and girls as agents whose dignity is central to it.

Responsibility for protection

Who has responsibility for respecting, protecting and fulfilling the sexual and reproductive rights of the Venezuelan women and girls who became 'necessary fleers' into neighbouring states? To address this question, we will start by considering how responsibility for human rights should be addressed, before turning to the question of how responsibility for the protection of the human rights of forcibly displaced persons should be conceived and distinguishing a range of different responsibilities in play in such protection.

Human rights may be conceived as denoting the membership conditions of global political society, recognizing that we inhabit a global political order which is structured as an international order of states and committed to securing human rights: 'Everyone is entitled to a social and international order in which the rights and freedoms set forth in this Declaration can be fully realized.' (UDHR, Article 28) Working to realize such a 'social and international order' and the responsibility to secure human rights is a duty that falls on global political society as a whole. Part of this duty of securing human rights is creating and sustaining the material and practical conditions of respect for, protection of and fulfilment of human rights – and it is this which we find articulated not only in, for example, international human rights law, refugee law, and the Migration and Refugee Compacts, but also in SDGs as key specifications of the requirements for states to be able to protect and fulfil the human rights of persons under their jurisdiction.

How is this duty to be discharged in an international order of states? It is important here to distinguish negative and positive duties:

> Negative duties – duties not to deprive people of what they have rights to are, and must be, universal. A right could not be guaranteed unless the negative duties corresponding to it were universal, because anyone who lacked even the negative duty not to deprive someone of what she has rights to would, accordingly, be free to deprive the supposed right-bearer. … The positive duties

> are the problem that feels severe because they involve the expenditure of resources already in one's possession, even if, where the duties are genuine, one is not actually entitled to keep those resources for oneself and, more important, because whatever proportion of the money, time, and energy currently at one's disposal one actually owes to others, the total amount one can owe to others must be limited simply because one's total resources are limited. (Shue 1988: 690)

On the basis of this distinction, Shue notes:

> Universal rights … entail not universal duties but full coverage. Full coverage can be provided by a division of labor among duty-bearers. All the negative duties fall upon everyone, but the positive duties need to be divided up and assigned among bearers in some reasonable way. Further, a reasonable assignment of duties will have to take into account that the duties of any one individual must be limited, ultimately because her total resources are limited and, before that limit is reached, because she has her own rights, which involve the perfectly proper expenditure of some resources on herself rather than on fulfilling duties toward others. (1988: 690)

In the international order of states, the first cut at ensuring full coverage of human rights in a way that is compatible with the autonomy of states is by allocating primary responsibility to states for protecting and fulfilling the human rights of their own citizens. However, this first cut is insufficient because, on the one hand, states may lack the capacity and/or disposition to protect and fulfil the human rights of their citizens and, on the other hand, states exercise jurisdictional authority over all who inhabit their territory whether citizens or not. Full coverage thus requires the construction or maintenance of international institutions that:

(a) encourage and enable states to protect and fulfil the human rights of their citizens and of non-citizens present within their territory; and
(b) make available human rights protection (in ways compatible with the normative structure of international order) when the state(s) with primary responsibility are unwilling or unable to do.

The duty to provide protection to those who become necessary fleers is thus derivative of the wider duty to ensure full coverage of human rights in global political society and is triggered by failures in the initial scheme of full coverage based on a division of labour between states. The content of this duty can be understood in terms of the principles of protection addressed in the previous section and, as we will see, this has implications for how responsibility for the protection of necessary fleers should be divided between states (and other actors).

We should note, first and foremost, that the duty of protection imposes a duty of cooperation on all states in discharging the duty of protection to necessary fleers.[1] As part of this duty of cooperation, states are obliged to construct, maintain or enhance institutions and organizations that can ensure that the principles of protection can be realized in ways that fairly share the responsibilities of protection between states. Considered in abstract and general terms, in relation to responsibilities for provision of places of protection, conditioned by the strict duty of non-refoulement, a range of normative criteria are pertinent, including crucially:

- the integrative capacity of individual states or regional association of states; and
- the legitimate interests of necessary fleers in seeking safety and conditions of effective social agency in particular state(s) or region(s).

With regard to schemes for allocating costs or resourcing, we can point to the duties of states in regional and international contexts to construct (adequately funded and resourced) institutions that enable:

- the provision of protection in the relevant places of protection; and
- conditions of mobility and voice for necessary fleers.

Other things being equal, the cost demands on states will be proportional to their capacity to supply resources or funds.[2] It is fairly straightforward to see how these two dimensions of the duty to protect necessary fleers interact. Thus, for example, the integrative capacity of a state is, in part, conditional on the ways in which its intrinsic capacity is supplemented and augmented through the provision of resources via regional or international organizations. The degree to which the legitimate interests of necessary fleers in having a say over where they seek settled protection is, in part, conditional on the degree to which their voice is recognized within these institutions and the range of mobility options made available to them by these institutions.

This discussion has, however, operated at a rather high level of abstraction and generality, and it is time to bring it back down to earth and to make it more precise by recognizing that in relation to any given mass displacement, the specific responsibilities of protection owed by particular states will be a function of their relationships with the context of displacement as well as with other states. We need to distinguish here between various types of responsibilities of protection:

- responsibilities for supporting *safe passage to places of first protection*;
- responsibilities for providing *places of first protection*;
- responsibilities for providing *safe mobility*;
- responsibilities for providing *places of settled protection*; and
- responsibilities for providing *resources for protection*.

Addressing these different responsibilities and their implications for how responsibilities should be shared in relationship to the specific context of Venezuelan women and girls and their particular interest in sexual and reproductive rights will provide a concrete way of illustrating the nature of these responsibilities and their distribution across states and the role of other actors within the domain of protection.

Responsibility, gender and the Venezuelan displacement

In this section, we work through the different types of responsibility and their implications in relation to displaced Venezuelan women and girls and their particular interest in sexual and reproductive rights.

Safe passage to places of first protection

We have already noted that, in a world of territorial states, safe passage across a border to a place of first refuge is crucial to any scheme of protection. The duty of protection and the duty of cooperation to which it gives rise thus generate specific obligations on states to whom direct passage is available as potential states of first refuge. The primary duty of such states is to keep their borders open to necessary fleers where this means that they do not prevent or obstruct such persons from accessing their territory to claim protection. It is easy in contexts such as the Venezuelan case to picture this in terms of women and girls walking or travelling by bus or car to the border and being confronted by border guards who refuse entry or demand documents as a condition of entry, and hence to think of the duty as one of simply admitting without such demands – and for many Venezuelan women and girls this will be the relevant way to envisage the duty. But we should further note that, at least once the dire nature of the situation in Venezuela is clear, this duty also encompasses allowing women and girls (who have the relevant financial resources) to access airflight to other states without being subject to visa demands that obstruct their travel.

It is, however, important to note that this duty also applies to the state from which flight is occurring. Apart from the negative duty not to prevent people seeking to leave its territory from doing so (expressed in the human right to leave, UDHR, Article 13.2), this state also has a positive duty to its citizens and residents to support their ability to travel safely to the border and to cooperate with other states in ways that support safe passage across the border. Of course, in cases in which the state is not disposed to protect the rights of the relevant citizens or residents, this duty is liable to be breached alongside others (although even here some local authorities or municipalities may be able to act differently than the central state apparatus); but in cases where the state lacks the capacity for protection, it may still be able to support safe passage and to the extent that it can, it has a responsibility to do so. What might this mean in practice? If we consider Venezuelan women and girls confronting the risks of travel to the border, we can distinguish three scenarios: *Open Border*, *Regulated Border*, and *Closed Border*. In the case of *Open Border*, where the potential state of first refuge is complying with the duty of cooperation for protection, the role of the Venezuelan state is to do what it reasonably can do to ensure that women and girls can travel in ways that are safe and secure from sexual assault or exploitation. This may include measures from providing information on how to travel safely to the designation of some services of the scheduled public transport to the border as 'female only'. In the case of *Regulated Border*, where the potential state of first refuge is not yet or not fully complying with the duty of cooperation for protection, the role of the Venezuelan state is, first, to communicate to, say, Colombia that the situation of the women and girls leaving is one of necessary flight so that the border should be opened to them and to provide whatever documentary support it can to those seeking to leave in order to enable them to meet the regulations currently in place. In the case of *Closed Border*, where the potential state of first refuge is wholly non-compliant with the duty of cooperation for protection, the responsibility of the international community, including the Venezuelan state, is to draw international attention to this noncompliance and may extend, depending on whether other states of potential first refuge are available and its relevant capacities, to ensuring that women and girls can access a state of first refuge, as well as to the need of increased availability of visa-free airflight routes.

Apart from the state from which flight is taking place and the state(s) to which the women and girls are fleeing, who else may have responsibilities with respect to safe passage? At least two other groups may have responsibilities in contexts such as the Venezuelan one.

The first group encompasses UNHCR, IOM, and humanitarian aid organizations. Their first responsibility is to use their available networks to communicate the conditions in Venezuela to states and other actors to make clear that conditions of necessary flight for women and girls are in place, and to communicate with women and girls in Venezuela concerning the conditions of passage and reception available to them. Insofar as they are able to operate within Venezuelan territory, a second responsibility is to provide medical resources and the provision of mobile/pop-up SRH clinics situated on the main travelling routes and near the main crossing places in order to address the health challenges identified by the women and girls themselves, for example, sanitary towels, contraceptive methods, prenatal control, treatment and prevention of STIs as well as trauma treatment and support (see Figure 4.1, Chapter 4). As we will claim, in addition to the delivery of these services in loco, the role of UN organizations should also be central as agents 'lobbying' for change by making, and operationalizing, these responsibilities into regional and international agendas such as the Refugee Compact.

The second group is that of the women and girls themselves. Here we can distinguish two responsibilities, each of which may be thought of as responsibilities of solidarity. The first is a responsibility of solidarity-in-transit, that is, a responsibility to support each other to the extent that they reasonably can do so through advice, self-organization and material aid. The second is a responsibility of solidarity-at-a-distance, namely, to the extent to which they reasonably can, to communicate their knowledge based on lived experience and shared communication with other fleers concerning the process of passage and their reception in the state of first refuge to women and girls who remain in Venezuela, either directly through their own networks or via humanitarian organizations, so that those who remain are able to make informed decisions about whether to leave, how to leave, and where to go. (It should be needless to say that states should not prevent or attempt to criminalize women performing solidarity-at-a-distance.)

Places of first protection

Responsibilities for providing places of first protection fall on all states to whom necessary fleers travel. The presence of necessary fleers on the territory of a state triggers a specific set of responsibilities of first protection on the part of that state as the representative territorial agent of the international community with respect to a specific set of forcibly displaced persons. In the first instance, these responsibilities involve providing safety (which involves both the strict duty of non-refoulement and protection in place), a fair and impartial process of status determination (although this latter step can often be done on a group-based criterion in contexts of mass displacements such as Venezuela), and access to identity documents that will enable displaced persons to access the support that they need to rebuild their lives and experience themselves as effective social agents able to make choices about their future. As we have seen, however, there are important gender-specific features of providing a place of first refuge. In the case of Venezuelan women and girls, we can highlight the following specific responsibilities:

- The provision of genuinely safe temporary shelter. This means, first and foremost, having shelter for women and girls that does not leave them exposed to risks of sexual assault as, for example, is the case in the open structure of the shelters provided in the main cities of arrival in Brazil where beds are provided for those who are not traditional family groups in an open plan format with no security for women or girls sleeping alone other than what they can organize for themselves. It also means having access to shelter on a 24-hour basis, especially for women with children, to avoid the risks of being subject to sexual assault, or sexual recruitment and exploitation, that arise from having nowhere safe to be during the day.
- Access to individualized identity documents rather than only family documents that potentially tie women and girls to male partners or parents and may facilitate forms of control and abuse.
- Effective and secure access to sexual and reproductive health. This entails not only that there is capacity for the provision of SRH services to all the displaced women and girls and that they have, and know they have, the right to access these services, but that it is provided in a way that is respectful of them as displaced Venezuelan women and girls. This requires that it is sensitive to issues of gender, age, culture and the disorientation and trauma that displacement often involves. This responsibility also entails that provisions are put in place to redress the barriers to the access of protection and healthcare identified by migrant women and described in Figure 4.1.
- Organized voice and mechanisms of consultation and contestation. Support for displaced women and girls to organize themselves and exercise voice in relation to the

> practices of protection to which they are subject by being consulted about the operation of protection and being able to challenge it. This is to recognize the epistemic dignity of women and girls as agents who can offer credible, and often epistemically privileged, testimony concerning the operative practice of protection, and their moral dignity as agents with a right to justification concerning how they are governed by the practice of protection.

In general, responsibility for addressing issues of protection in places of first refuge is shared between the states of first refuge as the representative territorial agents of the international community and international organizations, most obviously UNHCR, as the nonterritorial representative agents of the international community. The responsibilities of states who are not states of first refuge with respect to this initial condition of first protection thus typically takes the form of indirect duties that are discharged by supplying funding and resources to UNHCR and related bodies (like IOM and UNFPA). However, in the case of Venezuela, there is also a regional dimension to this responsibility as a responsibility of solidarity between South American states who are differentially impacted by the Venezuelan crisis. The importance of this point becomes clear when we reflect in particular on the issue of effective and secure access to SRH. Recall the problems of maternal health capacity faced by municipalities in Colombia and Brazil when confronted by the mass displacement of Venezuelan women and girls – and the negative political effects of these problems on the condition of reception of female necessary fleers (see Chapter 4). It is likely to be difficult for any state confronting sudden and significant increases in demands on sexual and reproductive health services of the kind encountered with the Venezuela displacement to be able to respond effectively and efficiently nor is it reasonable to expect such a state to be able to maintain the kind of excess capacity that would be needed to do so. No doubt this problem can be partly addressed through the international support provided by UNHCR and related organizations such as Medecins Sans Frontieres. However, in a region such as South America, preparedness for contexts of mass displacement within the region is a shared responsibility that is arguably best addressed at the regional level. Making policies at the regional level, going beyond security concerns, not only offers a mechanism for cross-border exchange and cooperation, but also makes sense because some social problems, such as those related to migration, health and the environment, for example, are exacerbated or facilitated by regional developments and exchanges (Riggirozzi and Yeates 2015; Riggirozzi 2017). After all, in both health and migration as spaces of regional governance, regional organizations were beginning to act as agenda setters and facilitators of resource collection and allocation (Riggirozzi and Ryan 2022). In the current context, regional spaces and norms can provide an opportunity to improve and strengthen collective management by creating new opportunities for tangible policy outputs, as illustrated in Table 5.1.

A shared regional facility of this type should prioritize a gendered approach to regional displacement, not only but especially in times of crisis. For supplying the material resources required to support treatment and capacity in places of first protection there is an urgent need of funding and of strengthening health systems, which most Latin American governments cannot offer. Under non-ideal conditions in which regional organizations often face severe resources restrictions, developing a regional capability *is* a prudent strategy which requires political commitment and supportive and unfailing international finance from institutions such as the World Bank and the Inter-American Development Bank.

Safe mobility

While some necessary fleers may have good reasons to remain in or near the sites of their border crossing and/or municipal

Table 5.1: Roles of regional organizations and outputs

Roles of regional organizations	Recognized outputs
Creation of normative frameworks	Changing issue salience and/or discourse use
	Specific actions taken linked to existing migration frameworks
	Leading regional network for definition of specific/contextual problems
	Specific policy guidance at regional level
Locking-in national policy	Strategically act as lightening rod
	Set targets and milestones and mechanisms of accountability
Reallocation of resources	Supporting specialist policy networks
	Sharing expertise and pulling together knowledge and material resources
	Reallocate support regionally (technologies/finance/ administrative resources)
Establishment of dynamics of representation	Represent local concerns not addressed by national governments at international level (such as proposals at UN levels, including inputs at the WHO, SDG and Global Compacts)

Source: Adapted from Riggirozzi and Ryan (2022)

places of first protection (for example, indigenous groups who circulate back and forth across the border), many will have legitimate reasons for wishing to move on, whether within the state, the region or internationally, in order to engage in rebuilding their lives and communities or to address specific needs (such as health conditions or disabilities) that they have as a condition of such rebuilding. Aleinikoff and Zamore (2019) propose that necessary fleers should be granted an updated version of a Nansen passport that enables them to move freely between those states in the world who are disposed to comply with their duty of cooperation for protection. However, although we agree that making such mobility available to necessary fleers is an important part of recognizing their agency and restoring their autonomy, a modern version of the Nansen passport can pick out necessary fleers and make them targets of discrimination. In the South American context, addressing movement within and across states in the region might arguably be better handled through a general expansion of mobility rights tied to an emergent regional citizenship. The 2002 Residence Agreement between countries in the Mercosur regional alliance, for example, has regulated movement and social entitlements in the region since 2009 (Ceriani Cernadas 2018). States also committed to recognizing equality in health, education and labour rights, regardless of migration status. Although policies have been poorly implemented at national level and the Agreement failed to address the gendered rights of women and girls or to guarantee gender-responsive services for them, it provides a basis on which to build a form of regional citizenship of which mobility rights are a central component. For most displaced Venezuelans, this would provide a key part of the basis for rebuilding lives of dignity. But not for all. For some, the best way of rebuilding their lives might take the form of travelling further; for example, to join extended family members in the US, Canada, Europe or elsewhere beyond the South American region, and here a Nansen passport would have an important role to play.

Responsibility for providing safe mobility to Venezuelan women and girls is not merely a matter of providing mobility rights, it is also about protection from abuses ranging from exploitation to trafficking. In contexts in which necessary fleers lack access to safe shelter or to formal employment rights, women and girls are highly vulnerable to being exposed to such risks. However, precisely because these necessary fleers will typically experience the disorientation characteristic of forced displacement, lack the same resources of knowledge and know-how enjoyed by citizens of the state of first protection, and be highly motivated to start rebuilding their lives, they are also likely to be vulnerable to deception and abuse of trust. As put by Gabriela, a Venezuelan migrant in Brazil: "One is exposed in a place that one does not know, without money, one arrives and does not know the people and a person may arrive and offers you a job, or to take you further but, not all are good people" (Manaus, 8 June 2021).

Even in contexts where necessary fleers have access to employment rights, forms of deceptive employment offers and exploitation are far too common. For example, Elena, a transgender fleer in Brazil, recalled:

> 'I worked for three weeks taking care of an old lady for less than 30 reais [£5] per week and I didn't know then, but I later learned she was exploiting me. I worked for her from Monday to Saturday, and on Sunday I would take her to the church. Once, whilst waiting, a woman in the church asked how we were related and what my nationality was. When I told her how much I made in this job, she said this was labour exploitation, that this was not supposed to happen here. I said that for me that was normal, because I was unaware of what was permitted or not.' (Manaus, 20 July 2021)

The commonality of these experiences became evident in a focus group discussion, where one interviewee claimed: "It is very difficult for us women to get a job … sometimes they make you indecent proposals … in a way is as if they tell you 'either you accept the job or not' … mostly in informal jobs" (Pisciana, Manaus, 2 October 2021). Another one seconded,

> 'I had the experience of working in a bakery, and I have a 16-year-old daughter. When my boss saw her, he immediately wanted to hire her, something which you cannot do, she is a minor. And he said he was attracted to my daughter and all that, and I had to leave my job, I had to move away and I couldn't get another job, I ended up cleaning houses, selling anything, selling sweets in the streets.' (Yuritza, Manaus, 2 October 2021)

As IOM (2021b) reports, across Latin America, one of the greatest priorities is addressing issues affecting female migrants' vulnerability to labour and sexual exploitation, trafficking and gender-based violence as well as labour informality, while increasing their capacity to report such circumstances and access official information. Thus, alongside mobility rights, states also have a duty of special care to necessary fleers, and perhaps especially so to women and girls, that derives from the potential exploitation of their social disorientation and lack of local know-how (especially by those who manifest markers of trust). This responsibility can be seen as extending across and linking places of first protection and places of settled protection as the sites where women and girls need to be supported both in the general process of re-orienting themselves to a new environment and in the specific process of being alerted to the risks of trusting too easily and the potential signs to watch out for.

Places of settled protection

Whether necessary fleers remain near their places of first protection or travel further afield to begin rebuilding their lives, they need to be able to integrate safely. Given our stress on the importance of mobility rights, especially regional mobility rights, as enabling the legitimate interests of those who are forcibly displaced to determine where they settle, we are proposing that, for most of those displaced, the region in general should be taken as the overall place of settled protection in which necessary fleers have access to the basic conditions for rebuilding their lives in community with others. However, women and girls will settle in specific places and it is necessary that resources travel with them.

What is needed for rebuilding lives in community? To adapt salient remarks from Owen (2020), we can say that the loss of effective citizenship experienced by those who have fled Venezuela can be conceived as the loss of reasonable conditions of effective social agency. To repair this situation means providing necessary fleers with conditions under which they can reasonably experience themselves as effective social agents, who can make choices and plans about their futures that are not simply driven by the urgent requirements of practical necessity and who have some ability to shape the social environment in which those choices and plans are made. The basic requirements of this responsibility can be expressed as provision of access to housing, health and welfare systems to protect necessary fleers from the overwhelming demands of practical necessity; of access to opportunities for education, training or employment to enable them to make effective choices and plans about their lives; and of access to municipal political membership to enable them to experience themselves as having some say over the environment in which they are situated. Each of these provide routes of social integration for necessary fleers within the place of settled protection but the second and third are particularly important as involving the active participation of necessary fleers in the social and political community of the locality in which they are situated. A scheme that denied them the opportunity for participation in education or employment and for local political participation would not only severely limit the ability of necessary fleers to experience themselves as effective social agents, it is also liable to support a demeaning picture of them among citizens of the place of settled protection as passive victims, civic burdens who are not 'real people' anymore, or even as (undocumented, illegal) aliens regardless of legal status (see Reed-Sandoval 2020).

Provision of the support needed by necessary fleers in accessing housing, health, welfare, education, training, employment, political participation and social integration is obviously not costless and may put strain on local services. Hence the importance of resources and support for the places of settled protection moving with necessary fleers to address capacity issues in delivering safe integration. In contrast to the provision of immediate capacity uplifts in places of first protection, capacity-building support in places of settled protection will typically involve those providing it having state-specific knowledge and experience, and hence while the provision of fungible resources should be widely spread, responsibility for provision of non-fungible resources will fall on the state in which settled protection takes place.

It is important to note here that the provision of this support needs to be responsive to gender-specific features of access to the conditions of socially effective agency. Thus, to take one example, access to (affordable) childcare will be a significant factor in potentially shaping the access of women to education, training, employment and political participation. This is not, of course, something particular to displaced women, although it is of particular importance for them, and it links to the gender-specific dimensions of sustainable development and social justice. In this respect, we might further argue that socially effective agency can be significantly supported by access to inclusive women's organizations in the place of settled protection which can act as a method of social integration and social empowerment for displaced women.

Resources for protection

Protection requires a range of resources and construed in abstract and general terms 'resources' would include the places where protection is carried out. However, we use the concept of 'resources' here in a narrower sense to refer to financial resources and to goods and services needed to secure protection. Our reflections on the various goods and services involved protection in safe passage, places of first protection, safe mobility, and places of settled protection have drawn attention to the fact that these goods and services require place-based provision by local, national and regional actors, supplemented (where possible given the nature of the good or service in question) by international organizations. The key issue here is capacity to provide the goods and services required for protection. Capacity is not reducible to considerations of cost but it is significantly related to them, and hence it is important to re-stress the point that the duty of providing protection for necessary fleers is a duty that falls on the international community as a whole, and a core part of the fair sharing of this responsibility involves recognizing that, other things being equal, states have a responsibility to contribute to the costs of providing protection according to their capacity to do so. Of course, those states that are providing places of first protection or settled protection are already contributing in place-based ways to some degree or other and hence the costs that they bear in doing so count towards their overall contributory obligations. Apart from place-based contributions, however, the primary route for discharging responsibilities for the costs of protection will be through the resourcing of international organizations such as UNHCR.

Here, however, we confront the fact that international protection is significantly under-resourced. As Aleinikoff and Owen (2022: 11) note:

> Each year UNHCR constructs a 'needs-based budget' by examining the needs of displaced populations around the globe and then calculating the amount of money it would take to enable such populations to lead lives at minimum levels of health, welfare and dignity. Actual funding for UNHCR never approaches that level; in any given year,

> UNHCR raises about 50 per cent of the 'needs-based' calculation. Likewise, the Office of the Coordination of Humanitarian Affairs publishes an annual 'global appeal' for funding necessary to respond to humanitarian emergencies; it too is dramatically underfunded each year. Data for 2020 showed global requirements at $38.5 billion, with actual funding reaching only $18.6 billion.

More specifically in relation to Venezuela, a UNHCR report in 2020 noted:

> UNHCR's overall requirements for the Venezuela situation in 2020 stand at $260.7 million. As of 25 August 2020, $68.7 million has been received. Flexible funds received by UNHCR have allowed the organization to allocate an additional $48.8 million to the Venezuela situation, raising the current funding level to 45 per cent. These low funding levels have forced UNHCR to cut programmes across a range of sectors, including child protection and livelihoods, with further cuts anticipated in the second half of 2020. (UNHCR 2020: 69)

Dupraz-Dobias (2022) gives a specific example of the effects of this shortfall:

> As of May 2020, due to funding shortfalls UNHCR was only able to support 50 vulnerable Venezuelan households in Antioquia and Choco departments to strengthen their access to livelihoods through the Graduation Approach, instead of the 1,200 households planned for 2020. According to UNHCR's Rapid Livelihoods Assessment, 67 per cent of Venezuelans in Colombia have lost all source of income since the onset of the COVID-19 pandemic in March, leaving them at increased risk of exploitation, SGBV, eviction and health challenges.

This shortfall takes on further significance when we note that in the absence of adequate funding, and in the context of rising poverty due to the COVID-19 pandemic, the likelihood of violence involving drug gangs and armed groups in Colombia increases despite a landmark peace agreement in 2016. In this context, Venezuelan migrants must compete for attention with Colombia's own internal crises. The UN's emergency aid coordination body, OCHA, estimates that 7.7 million people in Colombia – not including the Venezuelans – are in need of humanitarian assistance.[3]

The 2022 *Regional Refugee and Migrant Response Plan* by the Inter-Agency Coordination Platform for Refugees and Migrants from Venezuela estimates that $1.79 billion is required to address humanitarian assistance needs, but there is little reason to suppose that actual funding will be anything like the required level. Furthermore, even at this level of funding, what it is also and fundamentally needed is supportive and unfailing international finance for long-term sustainable development in ways that safeguards displaced women and girls' rights, fosters inclusive societies and redresses protracted inequalities for all.

Protection failures and responsibilities of development

What implications follow from the failure of the international community to provide adequate resourcing for protection? In pragmatic terms, the funding shortfall increases the strain on states of first protection and of settled protection – and such strain is liable to have political consequences in opening opportunities for politicians to frame social problems with these states in terms of the burdens of protecting displaced Venezuelans, particularly in contexts of social instability and economic austerity. Mitigating such strains and limiting the purchase of opportunities for a nationalist politics and discriminatory and exploitative situations can be addressed by intensifying international and regional cooperation and solidarity – with the caveat that regions in developing countries often already face a range of development challenges. Reflecting on this injustice also alerts us to the fact that the failure to fund protection adequately is not only a protection issue: it also has significant implications for the ability of the states of protection to make or maintain progress towards meeting SDGs and, especially significantly here, those SDGs which concern gender equality and gender justice. This particularly encompasses targets related to SDG 3 to achieve universal health and wellbeing, and to ensure universal access to sexual and reproductive health care services, including services for family planning, information and education, and the integration of reproductive health services into national strategies and programmes (3.7); SDG 5 on gender equality (5.2, 5.6), SDG 10 on reducing inequalities; SDG 11 on sustainable communities and goal 11.5 on protection of displaced people. Although many Latin American states have signed and ratified their commitments, the region continues to represent a major fault line for achieving these SDGs.

This recognition of the practical intersection of protection/humanitarian assistance of displaced people and development directs us to the important point that failures of responsibility for the costs of protection can generate special responsibilities of development aid, hence the call here for global partnerships and cooperation for development by mobilizing resources, sharing knowledge and building capacity in accordance with SDG 17.[4]

In other words, where funding for protection falls short of what is required with consequent negative effects on the capacity of protecting states to meet SDG targets, this calls for additional development resources to be provided for these states to repair the problems generated by the protection-responsibility failure. Notice that this special responsibility is not itself grounded in the claim to protection of necessary fleers, rather it is grounded in the claim of all who reside in a state and are subject to its authority not to be disadvantaged in relation to the state's capacity to achieve (or progress towards)

SDGs by the fact that the state complies with its responsibility to act as a state of protection to necessary fleers.

In practical terms, meeting the health needs of displaced people, particularly those of women and girls fleers, and ensuring their protection will require both emergency international funding ring-fenced for programmes that support healthcare, housing and social protection of people in displacement and that ensure an effective integration of migrants regardless of their legal status, and long-term investment in ways that is consistent with SDGs.

Here the role of World Bank and regional development institutions, such as the Inter-American Development Bank, are central for the funding of short and long-term programmes, while regional organizations such as Mercosur and the Economic Commission for Latin America and the Caribbean (ECLAC) are key for roles related to agenda-setting and creation of normative frameworks; supporting 'translation' of international norms into the local settings of states through regional networks of institutions; and enabling the mobilization of human, financial and knowledge resources in support of policy delivery. These tasks ultimately call for a 'new social compact', which was suggested by ECLAC in relation to health crises and amid COVID-19 for a recovery in the region.[5] A new social compact in the current context must contend with the gendered social and developmental consequences of mass displacement and health crises, where multilateral financial and development institutions adopt new modalities of immediate and long-term lending to ensure that international development aid programmes and funding are consistent with the SDGs and with the needs for practical and effective enactment of five types of responsibility identified here. These programmes must have a specific gender focus and boost national and regional organizations' capacities and roles. Finally, a system of accountability could support the new social compact by developing global performance indicators, complementary to or building on existing global indicator frameworks for the SDGs[6] or the COVID-19 Global Gender Response Tracker,[7] for example, to monitor responses taken by governments to tackle the five types of protection of displaced people. It would highlight those that have integrated a gender lens to protection and a gender-responsive approach to access to welfare, education and employment, and participation rights in the local community of displaced women and girls.

Taking seriously the dignity of displaced women and girls means addressing their access to human rights such as SRH rights and practically acknowledging the importance of their agency and voices within the governance of protection. But it also means recognizing the need to move beyond the protection framework to address the gendered conditions that generate necessary flight. One reason that adequate protection matters is that it enables displaced women and girls to act as agents of development in support of realizing SDGs. SDGs matter because they are integral to building a global basic structure that addresses the causes of necessary flight and its gendered characteristics.

Conclusion

In Chapter 2 we provided general conceptual reasons for adopting the necessary fleer framework to address the governance of protection for displaced persons in South America. These reasons were reinforced in Chapters 3 and 4 by attending the existing practices of governing access to protection and their failures as revealed in the lived experience of displaced Venezuelan women, and demonstrated the need for an ethics of forced displacement that would be responsive to the gendered character of such movement from the initial decision to flee through to the conclusion of the journey, whether it takes the form of settlement and integration or return. In this chapter, we have aimed to flesh out the character of such a robust ethics of forced displacement by delineating the varied responsibilities and forms of protection required across the different stages of displacement and identifying the diverse agents bearing these responsibilities. Our contextual analysis has indicated that discharging responsibilities for protection – and, in particular, gender-responsive forms of protection – requires action in concert by states, regional organizations, international agencies and non-state actors grounded in international and regional cooperation and solidarity. This is particularly important for moving beyond the kind of politics of ad hoc executive governance and its shortcomings illustrated in the preceding chapters and towards a stable rights-based structure of rule that secures protection and voice in protection to those displaced by actions and events beyond their control.

Conclusion

The gendered character of forced migration is brought into sharp relief by the mass displacement of Venezuelan women and girls. Not only are they compelled to flee for reasons that are typically either gender-specific (the collapse of maternal healthcare) or gender-inflected (as primary agents of familial care work), but they also confront gender-specific challenges in transit to, and reception and settlement in, countries of protection. Focusing on SRH provides a lens through which the gendered nature of their displacement and the necessity of gendered forms of protection is made visible even as it exposes a series of protection gaps that the failure to recognize the distinctive character of female forced migration generates.

The first and foremost of these gaps is the conceptual and normative failure of the protection regime to acknowledge that women and girls may have practically necessary reasons for flight not captured by legal conceptions of refugeehood. These conceptions are predicated on identifying this status with a limited range of specific causes or grounds of flight and hence with constructing the refugee–migrant binary in ways that allocate some forced migrants to one category and others to another. We have argued that addressing this conceptual failure and articulating a robust ethics of forced displacement can be accomplished by adopting Aleinikoff and Zamore's turn to the category of 'necessary fleer' and a framework of protection based on this status. We argue that the category of 'necessary fleer' distinguishes those who have compelling reasons of flight grounded in concern for protection of their basic rights from those who do not have such reasons of practical necessity. This combination of *generality* (in not tying international protection to specific grounds of flight) and *singularity* (in taking up the question of flight from the first personal perspective of the embodied agent faced with the practical question of whether to flee) overcome the conceptual and ethical problems posed by the migrant–refugee binary and disable the political uses of that binary. This provides us with a critical framework from which to reflect on the governance of forced migration in general and the governance of protection for Venezuelans in South America in particular, and to do so in a way that is sensitive to the gendered character of displacement.

Latin America may be seen as a privileged site for reflecting on the ethics of forced migration because it has been widely admired for its progressive legislation on refugeehood with the Cartagena Declaration being written into the domestic law of several states. However, the forced displacement of Venezuelan women and girls has drawn attention both to the limitations of that Declaration in addressing gendered causes of displacement (such as the collapse of maternal health systems) and to the ways in which South American states have aimed to address the mass inflow of displaced persons through political choices expressed in a range of measures that treated Venezuelans as migrants in need of temporary protection, practically limited access to refugee protection, and worked to consign many to a legally undocumented status whose effect was to position many more as socially undocumented (to borrow Reed-Sandoval's apposite distinction). This is not to deny or denigrate the very significant efforts made by states such as Colombia to address the needs of displaced Venezuelans within the constrained circumstances it confronts; rather it is to draw attention to the ways in which the absence of a robust ethical framework for addressing forced displacement, and especially gendered forms of forced displacement, at national, regional and international levels, acts as a facilitator of (often well-meaning) discretionary policies whose effects are to leave displaced women and girls without the protection that they require. Rather than a principled rights-based approach to the challenges of international protection, our analysis has found a series of more or less generous, more or less restrictive, ad hoc measures predicated on the use of discretionary executive powers. Rather than a rule-based framework that guides and coordinates local, national, regional and international responses, the practical actuality of the experience of Venezuelan necessary fleers more closely resembles a limited and restricted, often short term, 'care and maintenance' system. Moreover, as we have seen, ad hoc discretionary measures can generate different types of protection regime. They may differ in how they conceptualize protection leading to different views about what is required for the duty of protection to be met (ranging from provision of humanitarian basic needs to incorporation into society) and the scope of protection (to whom is protection owed and to what extent?) in ways that generate uneven access to protection. The examples of Brazil and Colombia illustrate both issues. The outcome is a significant practical gap between the promise of the progressive legal framework represented in claims of de facto protection to all forced migrants and the practical reality confronted by Venezuela necessary fleers. Our argument here highlights two points, one methodological and one substantive.

The methodological point is that the investigation and evaluation of protection regimes cannot sensibly operate at the level of general rights endorsed in constitutional, regional or international law, but must address how protection operates in practice on the ground. The task should make women and girls' voices heard, so that their specific needs and claims can be made known, and policies and protection regimes more broadly can be adapted accordingly.

The substantive point is that a secure regime of protection for necessary fleers is disabled by recourse to forms of migration governance based on the discretionary use of executive powers and highlights the need for a rules-based order that is ethically robust, limits scope for contingent political incentives to shape the governance of protection, and links municipal, national, regional and international responses in a common framework.

To address how protection operates on the ground entails engaging with how it is experienced by those who are subject to the regime of protection. Here our analysis used SRH as a privileged lens through which to address this issue and its gendered character. SRH is a central dignitary interest of women and girls, a fact recognized in a wide range of international conventions and agreements. Its importance justifies the choice of flight from a context in which it is not adequately available, as the Venezuelan displacement shows. However, SRH is also put at risk in the process of flight and may remain at risk in places of first or settled protection. The SRH rights of women and girl migrants and refugees are also important public health issues likely to have an impact on individual fleers as well as on population health. There are recognized synergies between good health and economic and social outcomes related to health. Yet, as we showed, opportunities and barriers of promoting and fulfilling the SRH rights of women and girls in displacement remain a challenge.

As the testimony of displaced Venezuelan women and girls makes clear, the forms of passage can vary along a continuum from relatively secure to extremely unsafe from an SRH perspective – and closures of borders in contexts of forced displacement heighten the risks of sexual assault, exploitation and trafficking to which female necessary fleers are exposed. Once they have arrived in the state of protection, their access to SRH rights confronts a range of barriers relating to, for example, status, documentation, language, culture, resources and employment. These barriers are created or exacerbated by the lack of gender-specific forms of protection that recognize that *what* protection is made available and *how* it is made available both need to address the distinctive needs of women and girls in displacement. Protection is a relational good in that its realization is a product of the relationship between, on the one hand, the services of protection provided and, on the other, the lived experience of access to these services on the part of those who require protection. Acknowledging this point highlights the importance of the inclusive participation of women and girls in the regime of protection. This is not only a way of acknowledging their dignity as subjects *of* protection (rather than merely being subject *to* protection) that has value in enabling their capacity for socially effective agency, it also has significant epistemic value as a critical feedback mechanism on whether the protection practices adopted by institutional agents are providing protection in a form that is effective and that successfully realizes its protective goals by being attuned to the needs-in-displacement of women and girls. Such needs-in-displacement – as our interviews with women and girls make clear – crucially include forms of respectfulness exhibited in being attentive to the gendered, linguistic and cultural dimensions of displacement. It is central to the effective provision of protection that those entitled to it do not experience themselves as being seen as merely a humanitarian problem to be managed by (a range of) institutional agents.

Protection of SRH is not, of course, just a matter of the effective provision of SRH rights in the form of generally available access to appropriately attuned medical services, it also hangs on the wider features of the regime of protection both in places of first safety and the places of settled protection. As our account of the various types of responsibility involved in a regime of protection and of the role of different agents in relation to these types of responsibility illustrates, the protection of SRH is bound up with the empowerment and integration of women and girls as socially effective agents. Yet as we have also highlighted, the resourcing of protection falls well short of what is required – and this points to a wider issue of global governance, namely, the failure to bring international protection and global development into genuine dialogue with each other. This failure is confirmed by 'the global evaluation [which] found significant gaps remaining, largely due to a lack of equitable and adequate funding dedicated to sexual and reproductive health services', particularly affecting humanitarian settings (Khosla et al 2019: 160).

Both the *Global Compact on Refugees* (GCR) and UNHCR acknowledged the urgent need for more equitable sharing of the burden and responsibility for hosting and supporting refugees, and the differential capacities and resources among states. Yet the GCR, a central framework guiding international response to large movements of refugees and protracted refugee situations, is not legally binding, and while defining principles of cooperation, it fails to mainstream effective sharing of responsibilities. There are three further consequences that affect taking forward effective commitments for shared responsibility in protection of displaced people, particularly women and girls, and durable solutions for their social, economic and political integration and agency 'in safety and dignity'.

First, the eligibility criteria under the applicable refugee definition, as provided for in international or regional refugee instruments, under UNHCR's mandate, and/or in domestic legislation overlooks conditions of practical necessity that make many forced to leave. Hence our claim that unless necessary fleers are protected on those grounds, the rights of displaced people will be ignored. There is recognition of 'refugee-like' conditions, but this ambiguous conceptualization supports further ambiguity in policy in refugee-hosting countries regarding who deserves to be protected and how. This also creates ambiguities in terms of how financial and development institutions, internationally and regionally, engage and support infrastructures of protection and social policy beyond emergency humanitarian action in response to migration 'crisis' and 'risks' rather than to the human rights of displaced people. There is therefore an unfulfilled yet urgent call for effective and sustainable cooperation and broadening the base of cross-border and transnational burden and responsibility sharing. While efforts in theory have been made to develop indicators to measure the volume of official development assistance provided to, or for the benefit of, refugees and host communities in the refugee-hosting countries, and other aspects of refugee-responsive policy,[1] unless these policies engage with broader commitments to respond to necessary fleers and unless the international community ring-fences appropriate resources for such sustainable response, existing declarations and theoretical commitments will remain all too nominal in practice.

Second, strengthening the response to gender-specific situations experienced by forcibly displaced women and girls requires supporting host communities and the displaced themselves. Little has been done to mainstream GCR recommendations into gendered responsive national policy, specifically in relation to access and fulfilment of SRH and rights, or to establish policies to hold states accountable to specific international and regionally gender targets. While the UN Deputy Secretary-General Amina Mohammed acknowledged in 2018 that 'refugees are among those furthest behind',[2] women fleers are particularly marginalized, isolated and made vulnerable due to unprotection. This is the situation, as we've explored, even the case in the states of Colombia and Brazil where 'progressive' policies and programmes have been put in place to respond to mass displacement from Venezuela.

Third, global aspirations for the health-related targets of the SDGs cannot be fulfilled without ensuring that all migrants and displaced people are able to realize their rights, including SRH rights. Yet while there is consistent rhetoric in relation to general goals for leaving no one behind, only one SDG (10) talks explicitly about refugees. While the GCR is particularly important to achieving the SDGs, there is no mainstreaming of developmental goals for state level policy implementation and funding strategies for international aid and humanitarian support, and certainly its guidelines lack a gender-focused.

As Denaro and Giuffré (2022) compellingly claim, the GRC and SDG frameworks seem to follow separate pathways related to goals to reducing poverty and inequalities, achieving universal health and wellbeing, and managing borders and surveillance. These goals signify a moving (policy) target, away from effective enactment of human rights-based policy and migration justice. Agencies of protection for refugees and the forcibly displaced, particularly women and girls, are in a privileged position to work with international aid agencies, regional organizations and national authorities in a new social compact, as we suggested in Chapter 5. This contract could bring these goals together and mainstream both policy and mechanisms of accountability to assess short- and medium-term gender-responsive measures to mitigate situations of humanitarian crisis and in long-term economic security, livelihoods and health of displaced women and girls in ways that safeguard their rights and opportunities to live lives of dignity.

Training a gendered lens on 'forced displacement' beyond the continuum 'migrant–refugee' and on women and girls' experiences, as we have done here, provides a deeper look at institutional, intersocietal and intersectional practices that not only reproduce gendered – and indeed intersecting – inequalities but fundamentally affect the exercise of rights of displaced populations. We have done so by bringing the voices of displaced women and girls into our analysis. Our contribution here is, therefore, threefold:

1) to approaches to the 'feminization' of migration, and specifically forced migration, that identify gendered vulnerabilities and inequalities;
2) to the study of displacement beyond state-centric approaches focused on migration management and beyond responsibility conceived as humanitarianism; and
3) to the contextual articulation of an alternative framework for identifying the duties of responsibility and protection that transcends the refugee–migrant binary.

In doing so, we identified key ethical and legal issues around broadening the scope of protection. Protection must be gender-responsive and recognize that any efforts to break cycles of deprivation and exclusion affecting displaced women and girls should privilege fulfilment of the right to health, particularly sexual and reproductive rights, as a determinant of sustainable development and social agency.

Notes

Introduction

1 Our analysis takes from the comprehensive definition of sexual and reproductive health and rights developed by the Guttmacher-Lancet Commission, which centres on: menstruation; contraception to prevent an unintended pregnancy; care for those who experience an unwanted pregnancy; prenatal, delivery and postnatal care for those who carry a pregnancy to term; and information and services for the prevention and management of sexually transmitted infections, and prevention and management of sexual and gender-based violence as central to this process (see Starrs et al 2018).

one The Gendered Character of Forced Migration

1 See Refugee Data Finder: www.unhcr.org/refugee-statistics/download/?url=pP3jV0

2 See UNHCR Refugee Data Finder: www.unhcr.org/refugee-statistics/download/?url=e7C00Y

3 General Comment 14: www.ohchr.org/sites/default/files/Documents/Publications/Factsheet31.pdf

4 The right to the highest attainable standard of health (Article 12 of the International Covenant on Economic, Social and Cultural Rights), p 10: https://documents-dds-ny.un.org/doc/UNDOC/GEN/G00/439/34/PDF/G0043934.pdf?OpenElement

5 *Trochas* is the word that migrants use to describe the irregular, alternative pathways used by Venezuelans and smugglers to cross the Venezuelan–Brazilian and Venezuelan–Colombian borders irregularly.

two Problematizing the Migrant–Refugee Distinction in Latin America

1 Henceforth the '1951 Convention' or 'the Refugee Convention'.

2 1951 Convention Article 1 A (2) and 1967 Protocol Article 1 (2).

3 See Feller et al (2003) for an overview of these developments.

4 Resettlement is the transfer of refugees from an asylum country to another that has agreed to admit them and grant them residence.

5 Besides the fact that Colombia has a very low rate of formal refugee recognition in general, among the places Venezuelans have fled to in Latin America (Argentina, Chile, Brazil, Peru, Colombia, Mexico, Ecuador, among others), only Brazil and Mexico have recognized a significant number of Venezuelans as refugees so far but, even there, they represent less than 50 per cent of the total numbers of Venezuelans in those countries.

6 Notice that this is not to say that all persons who are necessary fleers require, or should be entitled to, exactly the same form of protection. It may be, for example, the case that the protection of those threatened by state persecution requires more urgent access to citizenship in the state of asylum than those fleeing environmental disaster. But this is secondary for our current concern with the more general issue of access to international protection of basic human rights.

three Latin American Normative Frameworks of Migration and Asylum

1 Cartagena Declaration on Refugees, Colloquium on the International Protection of Refugees in Central America, Mexico and Panama, 22 November 1984: www.refworld.org/docid/3ae6b36ec.html

2 See Brazil Declaration: www.refworld.org/pdfid/5487065b4.pdf

3 For definitions, see 'Persons who are forcibly displaced, stateless and others of concern to UNHCR': https://popstats.unhcr.org/refugee-statistics/methodology/definition/

4 See data from Ministry of Justice, Brazil: www.acnur.org/portugues/wp-content/uploads/2018/01/refugio-em-numeros-2010-2016.pdf

5 These claims were made by public defenders, who issued a class action to suppress forced removals during the COVID-19 pandemic in 2020. See report of the Public Defender (in Portuguese), available from: www.mpf.mp.br/am/sala-de-imprensa/docs/decisao-liminar-impedimento-a-deportacao-de-migrantes

four Protecting the Human Right to Health of Women and Girls from Venezuela as Necessary Fleers

1 For information regarding normative and resolutions related to PEPs, see: www.migracioncolombia.gov.co/normativa/download/16-resoluciones-2017/70-resolucion-5797-pep-venezolano

five Responsibility and the Ethics of Forced Displacement in South America

1 Notice that this duty also applies to the state from which people are fleeing in that it imposes both negative duty on that state not to seek to prevent or obstruct necessary fleers from engaging in flight and, more specifically, from accessing the safest available forms of passage in travelling to and crossing the border to another state, and a positive duty to support safe passage when and to the extent it is able to do so.

2 However, other things are rarely equal, with some states often having played important roles in unjustly contributing to, or benefitting from, the structural or circumstantial conditions that lead instances of necessary flight (for example, the role of the US in Latin America over the past two centuries or so), and this justifies such states being subject to more demanding duties.

3 See Global Humanitarian Overview: https://gho.unocha.org/colombia

4 Goal 17 – Strengthen the means of implementation and revitalize the Global Partnership for Sustainable Development: https://sdgs.un.org/goals/goal17

5 See ECLAC's press release: www.cepal.org/en/pressreleases/eclac-proposes-political-and-social-compacts-broad-participation-more-symmetry-between

6 See indicators for SDGS: https://unstats.un.org/sdgs/indicators/indicators-list/

7 UNDP gender tracker: https://data.undp.org/gendertracker/

Conclusion

1 See *Global Compact on Refugees* indicator framework: www.unhcr.org/5cf907854.pdf

2 Press release DSG/SM/1247-HR/5419-IHA/1462, 17 December 2018: https://press.un.org/en/2018/dsgsm1247.doc.htm

References

Abubakar, I., Aldridge, R.W., Devakumar, D., Orcutt, M. Burns, R., Barreto, M.L. et al (2018) 'The UCL-Lancet Commission on migration and health: the health of a world on the move', *The Lancet*, 392: 2606–54.

Acosta Arcarazo, D. and Freier L.F. (2015) 'Turning the immigration policy paradox upside down? Populist liberalism and discursive gaps in South America', *International Migration Review*, 49(3): 659–96.

Acosta Arcarazo, D. and Geddes, A. (2014) 'Transnational diffusion or different models? Regional approaches to migration governance in the European Union and MERCOSUR', *European Journal of Migration and Law*, 16(1): 19–44.

Acosta, D. (2018) *The National Versus the Foreigner in South America: 200 Years of Migration and Citizenship Law*. Cambridge: Cambridge University Press.

Albaladejo, A. (2018) 'Contraceptive shortages mean Venezuela's people face a sexual health emergency', *BMJ* [online]. Available from: https://doi.org/10.1136/bmj.k1197 [Accessed 10 July 2021]

Aleinikoff, A. and Owen, D. (2022) 'Refugee protection: "Here" or "there"?', *Migration Studies* [online]. Available from: https://doi.org/10.1093/migration/mnac002 [Accessed 20 September 2022]

Aleinikoff, A. and Zamore, L. (2019) *The Arc of Protection: Reforming the International Refugee Regime*. Stanford, CA: Stanford University Press.

Amnesty International (2010) 'Widespread abuse against migrants is Mexican "human rights crisis"', press release [online]. Available from: www.amnesty.org/en/latest/news/2010/04/widespread-abuse-against-migrants-mexican-e28098human-rights-crisise28099/ [Accessed 10 July 2021]

Amnesty International (2018) 'Fleeing the country to give birth: the exodus of pregnant Venezuelan women' [online]. Available from: www.amnesty.org/en/latest/news/2018/05/huir-para-ver-la-luz-el-exodo-de-las-embarazadas-venezolanas/ [Accessed 10 July 2021]

Amnesty International (2022) 'Desprotegidas: violencia basada en género contra mujeres refugiadas venezolanas en Colombia y Perú' [online]. Available from: www.amnesty.org/es/documents/amr01/5675/2022/es/ [Accessed 10 September 2022]

Angulo-Pasel, C. (2018) 'The journey of Central American women migrants: engendering the mobile commons', *Mobilities*, 13(6): 894–909.

Arbel, E., Dauvergne, C. and Milllbank, J. (eds) (2014) *Gender in Refugee Law: From the Margins to the Centre* (1st edn). Abingdon: Routledge.

Asylum Access (2018) 'El derecho al trabajo de las personas solicitantes de asilo y refugiadas en américa latina y el caribe grupo articulador regional del plan de acción Brasil 2017' [online]. Available from: https://asylumaccess.org/wp-content/uploads/2019/07/Derechos-Laborales-Refugiadas-en-America-Latina-y-el-Caribe-final-ESP.pdf [Accessed 15 April 2022]

Awad, I. and Natarajan, U. (2018) 'Migration myths and the Global South', *The Cairo Review of Global Affairs* [online]. Available from: www.thecairoreview.com/essays/migration-myths-and-the-global-south/ [Accessed 11 April 2021]

Bahamondes, L., Laporte, M., Margatho, D., de Amorim, H., Brasil, C., Charles, C.M. et al (2020) 'Maternal health among Venezuelan women migrants at the border of Brazil', *BMC Public Health*, 20(1): 1771.

Bahar, D., Dooley, M. and Huang, C. (2018) *Integrating Venezuelans into the Colombian Labor Market: Mitigating Costs and Maximizing Benefits*. Washington, DC: Brookings Global Economy and Development.

Banco Mundial (2018) 'Migración desde Venezuela a Colombia: impactos y estrategia de respuesta en el corto y mediano plazo', *Colombia: Banco Mundial* [online]. Available from: https://openknowledge.worldbank.org/bitstream/handle/10986/30651/131472SP.pdf [Accessed 12 November 2021]

Barot, S. (2017) 'In a state of crisis: meeting the sexual and reproductive health needs of women in humanitarian situations', *Guttmacher Policy Review*, 17: 24–30 [online]. Available from: www.guttmacher.org/sites/default/files/article_files/gpr2002417_1.pdf [Accessed 12 November 2021]

Bastia, T. (2013) *Migration and Inequality*. London: Routledge.

Bastia, T. and Piper, N. (2019) 'Women migrants in the global economy: a global overview (and regional perspectives)', *Gender & Development*, 27(1):15–30.

Bauer, K. (2021) 'Extending and restricting the right to regularisation: lessons from South America', *Journal of Ethnic and Migration Studies*, 47(19): 4497–514.

Behrman, S. (2018) 'Refugee law as a means of control', *Journal of Refugee Studies*, 32(1): 42–62.

Beijing Declaration and Platform for Action (1995) *Resolution 1* [online]. Available from: www.un.org/womenwatch/daw/beijing/pdf/BDPfA%20E.pdf [Accessed 15 September 2022]

Bengochea, J., Cabezas, G., Gandini, L., Herrera, G., Luzes, M., Montiel, C. et al (2020) 'COVID-19 y población migrante y refugiada: análisis de las respuestas político-institucionales en ciudades receptoras de seis países de América Latina', in F. Vera, V. Adler and P. Ortiz (eds) *Inmigrando: Comprender Ciudades en Transición*. Buenos Aires: BID, pp 749–82.

Betts, A., Costello, C. and Zaun, N. (2017) *A Fair Share: Refugees and Responsibility Sharing*. Stockholm: Delmi [online]. Available from: www.delmi.se/en/publications/report-and-policy-brief-2017-10-a-fair-share-refugees-and-responsibility-sharing/ [Accessed 17 February 2023]

Bolivar, L. (2020) 'Acnur y los venecos', *Proyecto Micracion Venezuela* [online]. Available from: https://migravenezuela.com/web/articulo/acnur-y-los-venecos/1990 [Accessed 11 April 2021]

Bowser, D.M., Agarwal-Harding, P., Sombrio, A.G., Donald S. Shepard, D.S. and Harker Roa, A. (2022) 'Integrating Venezuelan migrants into the Colombian health system during COVID-19', *Health Systems & Reform*, 8: 1, DOI: 10.1080/23288604.2022.2079448.

Brandão, I. (2016) 'Roraima decreta emergência na Saúde por causa da imigração de venezuelanos', *Roraima* [online]. Available from: https://g1.globo.com/rr/roraima/noticia/2016/12/rr-decreta-emergencia-na-saude-por-causa-da-imigracao-de-venezuelanos.html [Accessed 11 April 2021]

Brazilian Declaration (2014) *A Framework for Cooperation and Regional Solidarity to Strengthen Protection of Refugees, Displaced and Stateless Persons in Latin America and the Caribbean*, UNHCR/ACNUR [online]. Available from: www.acnur.org/5b5101644.pdf [Accessed 19 September 2022]

Brumat, L. and Freier, F. (2020) 'South American *de jure* and *de facto* refugee protection: lessons from the South,' *ASILE* [online]. Available from: www.asileproject.eu/south-american-de-jure-and-de-facto-refugee-protection/ [Accessed 17 February 2023]

Brumat, L. and Finn, V. (2021) 'Mobility and citizenship during pandemics: the multilevel political responses in South America', *Partecipazione e conflitto*, 14(1): 322–40.

Bustreo, F. and Hunt, P. (2013) *Women's and Children's Health: Evidence of Impact of Human Rights*, World Health Organisation [online]. Available from: www.who.int/iris/handle/10665/84203 [Accessed 12 November 2021]

Cantor, D., Freier, L. and Gauci, J.P. (2015) 'Introduction: a paradigm shift in Latin American immigration and asylum law and policy?', in J.C. Cantor, J.P. Gauci and L.F. Freier (eds) *A Liberal Tide? Immigration and Asylum Law and Policy in Latin America*. London: School of Advanced Study, University of London, pp 1–10.

Cantor, D.J. (2013) 'European influence on asylum practices in Latin America: accelerated procedures in Colombia, Ecuador, Panama and Venezuela', in H. Lambert, J. McAdam, and M. Fullerton, M. (eds) *The Global Reach of European Refugee Law*. Cambridge: Cambridge University Press, pp 71–98.

CARE (2020) *An Unequal Emergency: CARE Rapid Gender Analysis of the Refugee and Migrant Crisis in Colombia, Ecuador, Peru and Venezuela* [online]. Available from: www.care-international.org/files/files/ENG_LAC_Regional_VZ_RGA_FINAL_compressed.pdf [Accessed 10 July 2021]

CARE and ODI (2014) 'Women, migration and development: Investing in the future' [online]. Available from: https://www.careevaluations.org/wp-content/uploads/Women-Migration-and-Development-Investing-in-the-future.pdf [Accessed 10 May 2021]

Caritas (2017) 'Children face hunger crisis in Venezuela as malnutrition soars'. Available from: https://www.caritas.org/2017/05/children-face-hunger-crisis-in-venezuela-as-malnutrition-soars/ [Accessed 21 July 2022]

Carreño-Calderón, A., Cabieses B. and Correa-Matus, M.E. (2020) 'Individual and structural barriers to Latin American refugees and asylum seekers' access to primary and mental healthcare in Chile: a qualitative study', *PLoS ONE*, 15(11): e0241153.

Cawthorne, A. (2014) '"*Pregnant*" schoolgirl display shocks Venezuelans', *Reuters* [online]. Available from: www.reuters.com/article/us-venezuela-mannequins-idUSKCN0IW26K20141112 [Accessed 12 November 2021]

Ceriani Cernadas, P. (2018) 'Migration policies and human rights in Latin America: progressive practices, old challenges, worrying setbacks and new threats', policy brief, Global Campus [online]. Available from: https://repository.gchumanrights.org/bitstream/handle/20.500.11825/629/PolicyBrief_LatinAmerica_ok.pdf [Accessed 12 November 2021]

Chant, S., Klett-Davies, M. and Ramalho J. (2017) *Challenges and Potential Solutions for Adolescent Girls in Urban Settings: A Rapid Evidence Review*. London: GAGE/ODI.

CIDH (Inter-American Commission on Human Rights) (2015) *Human Rights of Migrants, Refugees, Stateless Persons, Victims of Trafficking in Persons, and Internally Displaced Persons: Norms and Standards of the Inter-American Human Rights System (Human Mobility Report)*, OEA/Ser.L/V/II. Doc. 46/15 [online]. Available from: www.oas.org/en/iachr/reports/pdfs/humanmobility.pdf [Accessed 10 September 2022]

Cintra, N. (2020) 'Legal colonialism and migration law: between survival strategies and the illusory protection of the law', *Network for Migration Matters* [online]. Available from: www.networkformigrationmatters.com/brazilian-migration-law [Accessed 16 April 2022]

Collins, J. (2021) 'Closed borders aren't stopping Venezuelan migration, they're just making it more dangerous', *The New Humanitarian* [online]. Available from: www.thenewhumanitarian.org/news-feature/2021/5/27/hunger-and-COVID-19-drive-venezuelans-to-take-more-dangerous-routes-out [Accessed 10 September 2021]

Corte IDH (2020) *Cuadernillo de Jurisprudencia de la Corte Interamericana de Derechos Humanos No. 2: Personas en situación de migración o refugio/Corte Interamericana de Derechos Humanos y Cooperación Alemana (GIZ)*, San José, CR: Corte IDH [online]. Available from: www.corteidh.or.cr/sitios/libros/todos/docs/cuadernillo2.pdf [Accessed 16 April 2022]

Crawley, H. and Skleparis, D. (2018) 'Refugees, migrants, neither, both: categorical fetishism and the politics of bounding in Europe's "migration crisis"', *Journal of Ethnic and Migration Studies*, 44(1): 48–64.

Cubillos-Novella, A., Bojorquez-Chapela, L. and Fernández-Niño, J. (2020) *Situational Report: Venezuelan migrants in Colombia and the COVID-19 pandemic* (Spanish version), Lancet Migration [online]. Available from: https://1bec58c3-8dcb-46b0-bb2a-fd4addf0b29a.filesusr.com/ugd/188e74_dbcf1533c2994b47b039506a2cda3bde.pdf [Accessed 10 July 2021]

DataSUS (2020) *Brazil*, Ministry of Health [online]. Available from: http://www2.datasus.gov.br/DATASUS/index.php?area=0202 [Accessed 20 July 2022]

Del Real, D. (2022) 'Seemingly inclusive liminal legality: the fragility and illegality production of Colombia's legalization programmes for Venezuelan migrants', *Journal of Ethnic and Migration Studies*, 48(15): 3580–601.

Delgado Wise, R., Covarrubias, Márquez, H. and Puentes, R. (2013) 'Reframing the debate on migration, development and human rights', *Population Space Place*, 19: 430–43.

Dembour, M.-B. and Kelly, T. (eds) (2012) *Are Human Rights for Migrants? Critical Reflections on the Status of Irregular Migrants in Europe and the United States* (1st edn). Abingdon: Routledge.

Denaro, C. and Giuffré, M. (2022) 'UN Sustainable Development Goals and the "refugee gap": leaving refugees behind?', *Refugee Survey Quarterly*, 41(1): 79–107.

Do Carmo Leal, M., Gomes, T. and Portela Y. (2022) 'Changing demographics, risks and challenges of Venezuelan forced migrant women and girls in Brazil', research paper presented at the ACUNS Conference, 23–25 June 2022.

Doce, N. (2018) 'Venezuelan mothers-to-be head to Brazil to give birth', *Reuters* [online]. Available from: www.reuters.com/article/us-venezuela-migration-brazil-babies-idUSKCN1L713K [Accessed 22 April 2022]

Doña-Reveco, C. (2022) 'Chile's welcoming approach to immigrants cools as numbers rise', *Migration Information Source* [online]. Available from: www.migrationpolicy.org/article/chile-immigrants-rising-numbers [Accessed 22 April 2022]

Donato, K. and Gabaccia, D. (2015) *Gender and International Migration: From the Slavery Era to the Global Age*. New York: Russell Sage Foundation.

Doocy, S., Page, K., de la Hoz, F. and Spiegel, P. (2019) 'Venezuelan migration and the border health crisis in Colombia and Brazil', *Journal on Migration and Human Security*, 7(3): 79–91

Dupraz-Dobias, P. (2022) 'Nowhere left to turn, part 2: in a region hit hard by COVID, the welcome for Venezuelan migrants wears thin', *The New Humanitarian* [online]. Available from: www.thenewhumanitarian.org/analysis/2022/07/14/South-America-Venezuelan-migrants-COVID [Accessed 22 April 2022]

Economic Commission for Latin America and the Caribbean (ECLAC) (2000) 'International migration and development in the Americas', Symposium on International Migration in the Americas, San José de Costa Rica [online]. Available from: https://repositorio.cepal.org/bitstream/handle/11362/6533/S017586_en.pdf [Accessed 22 May 2022]

Feller, E., Volker, T. and Nicholson, F. (2003) *Refugee Protection in International Law: UNHCR's Global Consultations on International Protection*. Cambridge: Cambridge University Press.

Fernandes, A, and Jubilut, L. (2018) 'A atual proteção aos deslocados forçados da Venezuela pelos países da América Latina', in R. Baeninger and J.C. Jarochinski Silva (eds) *Migrações Venezuelanas*. Campinas: NEPO/Unicamp, pp 164–77.

Fernandes, V. and Oliveira V. (2021) 'PF invade brigo com mais de 50 mulheres e crianças venezuelanas em RR e ação cobra indenização por danos morais', *G1 Roraima* [online]. Available from: https://g1.globo.com/rr/roraima/noticia/2021/03/18/pf-tenta-deportar-mais-de-50-mulheres-e-criancas-venezuelanas-de-abrigo-em-rr-e-acao-cobra-indenizacao-por-danos-morais.ghtml [Accessed 22 April 2022]

Fitzgerald, D. (2019) *Refuge Beyond Reach: How Rich Democracies Repel Asylum Seekers*. Oxford: Oxford University Press.

Fleischman Y., Willen, S., Davidovitch, N. and Mor, Z. (2015) 'Migration as a social determinant of health for irregular migrants: Israel as case study', *Social Science and Medicine*, December, 147: 89–97.

Freedman, J. (2010) 'Mainstreaming gender in refugee protection', *Cambridge Review of International Affairs*, 23(4): 589–607.

Freedman, J. (2016) 'Sexual and gender-based violence against refugee women: a hidden aspect of the refugee "crisis"', *Reproductive Health Matters*, 24(47): 18–26.

Freedman, J. (2017) 'Women's experience of forced migration: gender-based forms of insecurity and the uses of "vulnerability"', in J. Freedman, Z. Kivilicim and N. Ozgur Bakacioglu (eds) *A Gendered Approach to the Syrian Refugee Crisis*. London: Routledge, pp 125–41.

Freier, L.F., Berganza, I. and Blouin, C. (2022) 'The Cartagena refugee definition and Venezuelan displacement in Latin America', *International Migration*, 60(1): 18–36.

G1 Roraima (2016) 'Justiça Federal em Roraima suspende deportação de 450 venezuelanos' [online]. Available from: https://g1.globo.com/rr/roraima/noticia/2016/12/justica-federal-em-roraima-suspende-deportacao-de-450-venezuelanos.html [Accessed 21 July 2022]

Garbett, A., Cintra, N., Riggirozzi, P. and Neal, S. (2022) 'The paradox of choice in the sexual and reproductive health and rights challenges of south-south migrant girls and women in Central America and Mexico: a scoping review of the literature', *Journal of Migration and Health*, Dec(7): 100143, DOI: 10.1016/j.jmh.2022.100143.

García, L. (2019) 'Estándares del Sistema Interamericano de Derechos Humanos sobre garantías del debido proceso en el control migratorio', *Estudios De Derecho*, 77(169): 119–44.

Gostin, L.O., Monahan, J.T., Kaldor, J., DeBartolo, M., Friedman, E.A., Gottschalk, K. et al (2019) 'The legal determinants of health: harnessing the power of law for global health and sustainable development', *The Lancet*, 393(10183): 1857–910.

Gerard, A.F. and Pickering, S. (2014) 'Gender, securitisation and transit: refugee women and the journey to the EU', *Journal of Refugee Studies*, 27(3): 338–59.

Grugel, J. and Riggirozzi, P. (2012) 'Post-neoliberalism in Latin America: rebuilding and reclaiming the state after crisis', *Development and Change*, 43: 1–21.

Guerra, K. and Ventura, M. (2017) 'Bioética, imigração e assistência à saúde: tensões e convergências sobre o direito humano à saúde no Brasil na integração regional dos países', *Cadernos Saúde Coletiva*, 25(1): 123–29.

Hamlin, R. (2021) *Crossing: How We Label and React to People on the Move*. Stanford, CA: Stanford University Press.

Hammoud-Gallego, O. and Freier, L. (2022) 'Symbolic refugee protection: explaining Latin America's liberal refugee laws', *American Political Science Review*, 1–20.

Hennebry, J.L. and Petrozziello, A.J. (2019) 'Closing the gap? Gender and the global compacts for migration and refugees', *International Migration* [online]. Available from: https://onlinelibrary.wiley.com/doi/epdf/10.1111/imig.12640 [Accessed 21 July 2021]

Herrera, G. (2013) 'Gender and international migration: contributions and cross-fertilizations', *Annual Review of Sociology*, 39: 471.

Ho, S., Javadi, D., Causevic, S., Langlois, E.V., Friberg, P. and Tomson, G. (2019) 'Intersectoral and integrated approaches in achieving the right to health for refugees on resettlement: a scoping review', *BMJ Open*, 9(7):1–13.

Hujo, K. (2019) 'A Global Social contract: new steps towards a rights-based approach to migration governance?' *Global Social Policy*, 19(1–2): 25–8.

Inter-American Court of Human Rights (2003) Juridical Condition and Rights of the Undocumented Migrants, Advisory Opinion OC-18/03 of September 17, Series A No. 18, para. 112.

International Organization for Migration (IOM) (2018a) 'Migration trends in the Americas' [online]. Available from: https://robuenosaires.iom.int/sites/g/files/tmzbdl626/files/documents/Tendencias_Migratorias_Nacionales_en_Americas__Venezuela-EN_Septiembre_2018.pdf [Accessed 10 April 2022]

IOM (2018b) *World Migration Report* [online]. Available from: www.iom.int/sites/default/files/country/docs/china/r5_world_migration_report_2018_en.pdf [Accessed 10 September 2022]

IOM (2021a) 'DTM general report focused on refugee and migrants children, on a long stay or street situation', *IOM Mission in Colombia* [online]. Available from: https://displacement.iom.int/reports/colombia-dtm-focused-refugee-and-migrants-children-long-stay-or-street-situation [Accessed 11 April 2022]

IOM (2021b) 'Venezuela regional response: gender-based violence and risk factors for migrant and refugee women from Venezuela during the migration journey' [online]. Available from: https://dtm.iom.int/reports/venezuela-regional-response-%E2%80%94-gender-based-violence-and-risk-factors-migrant-and-refugee [Accessed 10 September 2022]

Jubilut, L. (2007) *O Direito internacional dos refugiados e sua aplicação no ordenamento jurídico brasileiro*. São Paulo: Método.

Katja, H. and Piper N. (2015) *Multiple Forms of Migrant Precarity: Beyond 'Management' of Migration to an Integrated Rights-Based Approach*, UNRISD event brief. Geneva: United Nations Research Institute for Social Development.

Khosla, R., Krause, S. and Tanabe, M. (2019) 'Addressing the rights of women in conflict and humanitarian settings', in P. Allotey and D. Reidpath (eds) *The Health of Refugees: Public Health Perspectives from Crisis to Settlement*. Oxford: Oxford University Press, pp 153–168.

Kneebone, S. (2019) 'Humanitarianism, refugees, human rights, and health', in: P. Allotey and D. Reidpath (eds) *The Health of Refugees* (2nd edn). Oxford: Oxford University Press, pp 19–38.

Krause, U. (2021) 'Colonial roots of the 1951 Refugee Convention and its effects on the global refugee regime', *Journal of International Relations and Development*, 24: 599–626.

The Lancet (2018) 'The collapse of the Venezuelan health system', *The Lancet*, 391(10128): 1331 [online]. Available from: www.thelancet.com/journals/lancet/article/PIIS0140-6736(16)00277-4/fulltext [Accessed 11 April 2022]

La Opinion (2018) 'Brasileños expulsan a venezolanos de campamentos y queman sus cosas', video [online]. Available from: https://laopinion.com/2018/08/19/video-brasilenos-expulsan-a-venezolanos-de-campamentos-y-queman-sus-cosas/ [Accessed 10 September 2022]

Lenard, P (2020) 'Seeking asylum during the pandemic: on why borders must remain a little open', Centre for International Policy Studies (CIPS) [online]. Available from: www.cips-cepi.ca/2020/04/22/seeking-asylum-during-the-pandemic-on-why-borders-must-remain-a-little-open [Accessed 10 September 2022]

Liberona, N. and Masilla M.A. (2017) 'Pacientes ilegítimos: acceso a la salud de los inmigrantes indocumentados en Chile', *Salud Colectiva*, 13: 507–20.

Luigi-Bravo, G. and Kaur Gill, R. (2022) 'Safe abortion within the Venezuelan complex humanitarian emergency: understanding context as key to identifying the potential for digital self-care tools in expanding access', *Sexual and Reproductive Health Matters*, 29(3), DOI: 10.1080/26410397.2022.2067104.

Madise, N. and Onyango, B. (2017) 'Protecting female migrants from forced sex and HIV infection', *The Lancet*, 3(1): E2–E3.

Makuch, M.Y., Osis, M.J.D., Brasil, C., de Amorim, H.S.F. and Bahamondes, L. (2021) 'Reproductive health among Venezuelan migrant women at the north western border of Brazil: a qualitative study', *Journal of Migration and Health*, 4(100060): 1–8.

Malo, M.G. (2020) 'Access to formal employment and mobility: Colombian and Venezuelan forced migrants in Ecuador', discussion paper [online]. Available from: https://sas-space.sas.ac.uk/9328/ [Accessed 10 September 2021]

Marillier, L. and Squires, D. (2018) 'Lacking birth control options, desperate Venezuelan women turn to sterilization and illegal abortion', *The Intercept* [online]. Available from: https://theintercept.com/2018/06/10/venezuela-crisis-sterilization-women-abortion/ [Accessed 11 April 2021]

Mármora, L. (2010) 'Modelos de gobernabilidad migratoria: la perspectiva política en América del Sur', *Revista Interdisciplinaria de Movilidad Humana*, 35, Year XVIII (July–December): 71–92.

Martin, S.F. (2010) 'Gender and the evolving refugee regime', *Refugee Survey Quarterly*, 29(2): 104–21. Available from: www.jstor.org/stable/45054457 [Accessed 11 April 2021]

McAdam, J. (2014) 'Human rights and forced migration', in E. Fiddian-Qasmiyeh, G. Loescher, K. Long and N. Sigona (eds) *The Oxford Handbook of Refugee and Forced Migration Studies*. Oxford: Oxford University Press, pp 203–14.

Medecins Sans Frontieres (2017) *Forced to Flee Central America's Northern Triangle: A Neglected Humanitarian Crisis* [online]. Available from: www.msf.org/sites/default/files/msf_forced-to-flee-central-americas-northern-triangle_e.pdf [Accessed 17 February 2023]

Medecins Sans Frontieres (2020) *No way out: The humanitarian crisis for migrants and asylum seekers trapped between the United States, Mexico and the Northern Triangle of Central America* [online]. Available from: www.msf.org/report-no-way-out-central-american-migration [Accessed 11 April 2021]

Menjívar, C. and Walsh, S.D. (2017) 'The architecture of feminicide: the state, inequalities, and everyday gender violence in Honduras', *Latin American Research Review*, 52(2): 221–40.

Metusela, C., Ussher, J., Perz, J., Hawkey, A., Morrow, M., Narchal, R., Estoesta, J. and Monteiro, M. (2017) '"In my culture, we don't know anything about that": sexual and reproductive health of migrant and refugee women', *International Journal of Behavioural Medicine*, 24(6): 836–45.

Meyer, S., Robinson, W., Branchini, C., Abshir, N., Mar, A. and Decker, M. (2018) 'Gender differences in violence and other human rights abuses among migrant workers on the Thailand–Myanmar border', *Violence Against Women*, 25(8): 945–67.

Moloney, A. (2019) 'As Venezuela's healthcare collapses, pregnant women, girls bear brunt of crisis', *Reuters* [online]. Available from: www.reuters.com/article/us-venezuela-health-women-idUSKCN1U32AS [Accessed 22 April 2022]

Moulin, C. and Magalhães, B. (2020). 'Operation shelter as humanitarian infrastructure: material and normative renderings of Venezuelan migration in Brazil', *Citizenship Studies*, 24(5): 642–62.

Muntaner, C., Salazar, R.M., Benach, J. and Armada, F. (2006) 'Venezuela's Barrio Adentro: an alternative to neoliberalism in health care', *International Journal of Health Services: Planning, Administration, Evaluation*, 36(4): 803–11.

Ní Ghráinne, B. (2020) 'Safe zones and the internal protection alternative', *International and Comparative Law Quarterly*, 69(2): 335–64.

Obach, A., Hasen, F., Cabieses, B., D'Angelo, C. and Santander, S. 'Conocimiento, acceso y uso del sistema de salud en adolescentes migrantes en Chile: resultados de un estudio exploratorio', *Rev Panam Salud Publica*, Dec 30(44): e175. DOI: 10.26633/RPSP.2020.175.

Office of the United Nations High Commissioner for Human Rights (OHCHR) (2018) *Human rights violations in the Bolivarian Republic of Venezuela: a downward spiral with no end in sight* [online]. Available from: www.ohchr.org/sites/default/files/Documents/Countries/VE/VenezuelaReport2018_EN.pdf [Accessed 11 April 2022]

OHCHR (2020) 'OHCHR guidance note: prohibition of evictions' [online]. Available from: www.ohchr.org/Documents/Issues/Housing/SR_housing_COVID-19_guidance_evictions.pdf [Accessed 17 September 2022]

Owen, D. (2018) 'Refugees and shared responsibilities of justice', *Global Justice*, 11(1): 23–44.

Owen, D. (2020) *What Do We Owe to Refugees?* Cambridge: Polity.

Owen, D. (2021) 'Solidarity and the politics of redress: structural injustice, history and counter-finalities', *Ethic Theory Moral Practice*, 24: 1213–27.

Pan-American Health Organization (PAHO) (2019a) *Gender Equality in Addressing the Causes and Consequences of the Health of Migrant Women*, technical report [online]. Available from: www.paho.org/hq/index.php?option=com_docman&view=download&slug=international-women-day-2019-technical-note-eng&Itemid=270&lang=en [Accessed 7 September 2021]

PAHO (2019b) 'Technical brief: gender equality in addressing the causes and consequences of the health of migrant women' [online]. Available from: www.paho.org/hq/index.php?option=com_docman&view=download&slug=international-women-day-2019-technical-note-eng&Itemid=270&lang=en [Accessed 7 September 2021]

Petrinioti, S., Tastsoglou, E. and Karagiannopoulou, C. (2021) 'The gender-based violence and precarity nexus: asylum-seeking women in the Eastern Mediterranean', *Frontiers in Human Dynamics*, 3(27). Available from: https://doi.org/10.3389/fhumd.2021.660682 [Accessed 11 May 2023]

Pierola, M. and Rodríguez Chatruc, M. (2020) *Migrants in Latin America: Disparities in Health Status and in Access to Healthcare*, discussion paper IDB-DP-00784. Washington, DC: InterAmerican Development Bank [online]. Available from: https://publications.iadb.org/publications/english/document/Migrants-in-Latin-America-Disparities-in-Health-Status-and-in-Access-to-Healthcare.pdf [Accessed 20 February 2023]

Piper, N. (2009) *Migration and Social Development: Organizational and Political Dimensions*, Social and Development Programme Paper 39. Geneva: United Nations Research Institute for Social Development.

Profamilia (2020) *Health Services Inequalities Affecting the Venezuelan Migrant and Refugee Population in Colombia: How to Improve the Local Response to the Humanitarian Emergency?* [online]. Available from: https://profamilia.org.co/wp-content/uploads/2020/06/Health-services-inequalities-affecting-the-Venezuelan-migrant-and-refugee-population-in-Colombia-how-to-improve-the-local-response-to-the-humanitarian-emergency.pdf [Accessed 10 September 2022]

R4V (2022) 'RV4 Latin America and the Caribbean, Venezuelan refugees and migrants in the region – February' [online]. Available from: www.r4v.info/en/document/r4v-latin-america-and-caribbean-venezuelan-refugees-and-migrants-region-february-2022 [Accessed 10 September 2022]

Reed-Hurtado, M. (2013) *The Cartagena Declaration on Refugees and the Protection of People Fleeing Armed Conflict and Other Situations of Violence in Latin America*, Geneva: UNHCR [online]. Available from: www.refworld.org/pdfid/51c801934.pdf [Accessed 10 September 2022]

Reed-Sandoval, A. (2020) *Socially Undocumented: Identity and Immigration Justice*. Oxford: Oxford University Press.

Restrepo, J.P., Jaramillo, J., and Torres, M. (2018) *Venezuelans in Colombia: Understanding the Implications of the Migrants Crisis in Maicao (La Guajira)*. Vienna, VA: SARAYA International.

Riggirozzi, P. (2021) 'Everyday political economy of human rights to health: dignity and respect as an approach to gendered inequalities and accountability', *New Political Economy*, 26(5): 735–47.

Riggirozzi, P., Curcio, B., Lines, T. and Cintra, N. (2023) *Moving Forward: Health, Care and Violence Seen Through the Eyes of Displaced Venezuelan Women in Brazil*. London: Latin American Bureau/Practical Action Publishing.

Riggirozzi, P. (2012) 'Region, regionness and regionalism in Latin America: towards a new synthesis', *New Political Economy*, 17(4): 421–43.

Riggirozzi, P. (2017) 'Regional integration and welfare: framing and advocating pro-poor norms through southern regionalisms', *New Political Economy*, 22(6): 661–75.

Riggirozzi, P. and Ryan, M. (2022) 'The credibility of regional policymaking: insights from South America', *Globalizations*, 19(4): 604–19.

Riggirozzi, P. and Yeates, N. (2015) 'Locating regional health policy: institutions, politics, and practices', *Global Social Policy*, 15(3), 212–28.

Riggirozzi, P., Grugel, J. and Cintra, N. (2020) 'Situational brief: perspective on migrants' right to health in Latin America during COVID-19', *Lancet Migration*, June [online]. Available from: https://1bec58c3-8dcb-46b0-bb2a-fd4addf0b29a.filesusr.com/ugd/188e74_543cbb0400824084abcea99479dfa124.pdf?index=true [Accessed 10 September 2022]

Rivillas, J.C., Devia Rodriguez, R., Song, G. and Martel, A. (2018) 'How do we reach the girls and women who are the hardest to reach? Inequitable opportunities in reproductive and maternal health care services in armed conflict and forced displacement settings in Colombia', *PLoS ONE*, 13(1): e0188654 [online]. Available from: https://journals.plos.org/plosone/article?id=10.1371/journal.pone.0188654 [Accessed 11 April 2022]

Rivillas-García, J.C., Cifuentes-Avellaneda, Á., Ariza-Abril, J.S., Sánchez-Molano, M. and Rivera-Montero, D. (2020) 'Venezuelan migrants and access to contraception in Colombia: a mixed research approach towards understanding patterns of inequality', *Journal of Migration and Health*, 11(3)100027: 1-10, DOI: 10.1016/j.jmh.2020.100027

Rosen, M. (2012) *Dignity: Its History and Meaning*. Cambridge, MA: Harvard University Press.

Roth, B. (2021) 'Temporary shelter: Venezuelan Migrants and the uncertainty of waiting in Colombia', *Journal of Immigrant & Refugee Studies*, DOI: 10.1080/15562948.2021.1974147.

Sahraoui, N. and Tyszler, E. (2021) 'Tracing colonial maternalism within the gendered morals of humanitarianism: experiences of migrant women at the Moroccan–Spanish Border', *Frontiers in Human Dynamics*, 3: 642326.

Selee, A. and Bolter, J. (2022) 'Colombia's open-door policy: an innovative approach to displacement?', *International Migration*, 60(1): 113–31.

Selee, A., Bolter, J., Muñoz-Pogossian, B. and Hazán, M. (2019) *Creativity Amid Crisis: Legal Pathways for Venezuelan Migrants in Latin America*. Washington, DC: Migration Policy Institute and Organization of American States [online]. Available from: www.migrationpolicy.org/research/legal-pathways-venezuelan-migrants-latin-america [Accessed 10 September 2022]

Shacknove, A. (1985) 'Who is a refugee?' *Ethics*, 95(2): 274–84.

Shue, H. (1988) 'Mediating duties', *Ethics*, 98(4): 687–704.

Shue, H. (1995) *Basic Rights: Subsistence, Affluence and US Foreign Policy*. New Haven, CT: Princeton University Press.

Soria-Escalante, H., Alday-Santiago, A., Alday-Santiago, E., Limón-Rodríguez, N., Manzanares-Melendres, P. and Tena-Castro, A. (2022) '"We all get raped": sexual violence against Latin American women in migratory transit in Mexico', *Violence Against Women*, 28(5): 1259–81.

Starrs, A.M., Ezeh, A.C., Barker, G., Basu, A, Bertrand, J.T., Blum, R. et al (2018) 'Accelerate progress – sexual and reproductive health and rights for all: report of the Guttmacher-Lancet Commission', *The Lancet*, 391(10140): 2642–92 [online]. Available from: www.thelancet.com/pdfs/journals/lancet/PIIS0140-6736(18)30293-9.pdf [Accessed 7 September 2021]

Surita, T (2020) 'Boa Vista, the early childhood capital, faces prejudice and Covid-19', *Early Childhood Matters* [online]. Available from: https://earlychildhoodmatters.online/wp-content/uploads/2020/11/ECM2020_Leadership_Boa-Vista-the-Early-Childhood-capital-faces-prejudice-and-Covid-19.pdf [Accessed 10 September 2022]

Tavares, N. and Cabral, V. (2020) 'The application of the Cartagena Declaration on refugees to Venezuelans in Brazil: an analysis of the decision-making process by the National Committee for Refugees', *Latin American Law Review*, 5: 121–37.

Telesur (2016) 'Cuba-Venezuela mission to prevent blindness helps 3.5 million' [online]. Available from: www.telesurenglish.net/news/CubaVenezuela-Mission-to-Prevent-Blindness-Helps-3.5-Million-20140722-0036.html [Accessed 22 April 2022]

Temin, M., Montgomery, M.R., Engebretsen, S. and Barker, K.M. (2013) *Girls on the Move: Adolescent Girls & Migration in the Developing World*, Population Council [online]. Available from: http://www.popcouncil.org/research/ girls-on-the-move-adolescent-girls-migration-in-the-developing-world [Accessed 7 July 2022]

Tinker, C. and Sartoretto, L. (2018) 'New trends in migratory and refugee law in Brazil: the expended refugee definition', *Panorama of Brazilian Law*, 3(3–4): 143–69.

UN Committee on the Elimination of Discrimination Against Women (CEDAW) (1999) *CEDAW General Recommendation No. 24: Article 12 of the Convention (Women and Health)*, A/54/38/Rev.1, chap. I [online]. Available from: www.refworld.org/docid/453882a73.html [Accessed 15 September 2022]

UN Women (2016) *Guide on Mainstreaming Migration into Development Planning from a Gender Perspective* [online]. Available from: www.unwomen.org/sites/default/files/Field%20Office%20ESEAsia/Docs/Publications/2016/10/UN%20WOMEN%20GUIDE%20ON%20MAINSTREAMING%207-27-16.pdf [Accessed 10 September 2022]

United Nations Population Fund (UNFPA) (2009) *A Companion to the Inter-Agency Field Manual on Reproductive Health in Humanitarian Settings*. New York: UNFPA.

UNFPA (2018) 'Cinco motivos por los que la migración es una cuestión feminista' [online]. Available from: www.unfpa.org/es/news/migración-feminista [Accessed 10 September 2022]

UNICEF (2021) *BRAZIL: Increased Migration Influx in Pacaraima Flash Situation Report No. 1* [online]. Available from: www.unicef.org/media/107836/file/Brazil-Flash-SitRep-28-September-2021.pdf [Accessed 7 July 2022]

United Nations (2006) 'Feminization of migration, remittances, migrants' rights, brain drain among issues, as population commission concludes debate', Session 39, UN Commission on Population and Development Press Release [online]. Available from: https://press.un.org/en/2006/pop945.doc.htm [Accessed 10 July 2021]

United Nations High Commissioner for Human Rights (2019) *Human Rights in the Bolivarian Republic of Venezuela*, UN Document: A/HRC/41/18 [online]. Available from: https://documents-dds-ny.un.org/doc/UNDOC/GEN/G19/301/92/PDF/G1930192.pdf [Accessed 20 February 2023]

UNHCR (1951) UN 1951 Convention Article 1 A (2) and 1967 Protocol, Article 1 (2) [online]. Available from: www.unhcr.org/uk/1951-refugee-convention.html [Accessed 7 July 2021]

UNHCR (1961) Brazil ratification of the 1951 Convention, Decree nº 50.215, of January 28th, 1961.

UNHCR (1972) Brazil ratification of the 1967 Protocol, Decree 70.946 of August 7th, 1972.

UNHCR (2001) *UNHCR Refugee Statistics* [online]. Available from: www.unhcr.org/refugee-statistics/download/?url=pP3jV0 [Accessed 10 July 2021]

UNHCR (2002) *UNHCR Policy on Refugee Women and Guidelines on Their Protection: An Assessment of Ten Years of Implementation* [online]. Available from: www.refworld.org/pdfid/48aa83220.pdf [Accessed 7 July 2022].

UNHCR (2005) *UNHCR's Age and Gender Mainstreaming Pilot Project: Synthesis Report*, EPAU/2005/03.

UNHCR (2013) *From 1975 to 2013: UNHCR's Gender Equality Chronology* [online]. Available from: www.unhcr.org/543b90796.pdf [Accessed 7 September 2021]

UNHCR (2016) *UNHCR Review of Gender Equality in Operations* [online]. Available from: www.unhcr.org/uk/protection/women/57f3b9a74/unhcr-review-gender-equality-operations-2016.html [Accessed 7 July 2021]

UNHCR (2017) *Achieving Gender Equality and Addressing Sexual and Gender-based Violence in the Global Compact on Refugees: Major Themes and Key Recommendations from the Five Thematic Discussions and the High Commissioner's Dialogue* [online]. Available from: www.unhcr.org/uk/5a72f2eb7.pdf [Accessed 7 July 2021]

UNHCR (2018a) *UNHCR Global Compact on Refugees* [online]. Available from: www.unhcr.org/5c658aed4 [Accessed 7 July 2021]

UNHCR (2018b) *Brazil Plan of Action: First Triennial Progress Report 2015–2017* [online]. Available from: www.refworld.org.es/pdfid/5c883e844.pdf [Accessed 20 February 2023]

UNHCR (2019) *Colombia Ficha Informativa* [online]. Available from: www.refworld.org.es/pdfid/5e69300f4.pdf [Accessed 11 April 2022]

UNHCR (2020) *Venezuela Situation* [online]. Available from: www.unhcr.org/underfunding-2020/wp-content/uploads/sites/107/2020/09/Underfunding-2020-Venezuela.pdf [Accessed 7 September 2022]

UNHCR (2021) *UNHCR Ecuador: Health* [online]. Available from: www.acnur.org/60b520094.pdf [Accessed 7 July 2022]

UNHCR (2022) 'Refugee Data Finder' [online]. Available from: www.unhcr.org/refugee-statistics/download/?url=e7C00Y [Accessed 7 July 2021]

Valdez, E.S., Valdez, L.A. and Sabo, S. (2015) 'Structural vulnerability among migrating women and children fleeing Central America and Mexico: the public health impact of "Humanitarian Parole"', *Frontiers in Public Health*, 3: 163.

Van Praag, O. (2019) 'Understanding the Venezuelan refugee crisis', Wilson Center [online]. Available from: www.wilsoncenter.org/article/understanding-the-venezuelan-refugee-crisis [Accessed 20 August 2022]

Vázquez-Quesada, L.M., Peña, J. and Vieitez-Martínez, I. (2021) *Necesidades y atención en salud sexual y reproductiva de mujeres migrantes en México. Un estudio desde Ciudad Juárez, Chihuahua*, Volumen I. Mexico: Population Council y El Colegio de la Frontera Norte.

Ventura, D., Martins da Silva, J., Calderón, L. and Eguiluz, I. (2021) 'Migration, migrants, and health in Latin America and the Caribbean', *Oxford Research Encyclopedia of Global Public Health* [online]. Available from: https://oxfordre.com/publichealth/view/10.1093/acrefore/9780190632366.001.0001/acrefore-9780190632366-e-323 [Accessed 20 August 2022]

Vera Espinoza, M., Jubilut, L. and Mezzanotti, G. (2021) *Latin America and Refugee Protection: Regimes, Logics, and Challenges*. Oxford: Berghan Books.

Waldron, J. (2012) *The Harm in Hate Speech*. Cambridge, MA: Harvard University Press.

Walsham, M. (2022) *Gender and Global Migration Governance for South-South Migration*, working paper, MIDEQ: Migration for Development and Equality, January [online]. Available from: https://southsouth.contentfiles.net/media/documents/Gender_and_Global_Migration_Governance_for_South-South_Migration_Working_Paper.pdf [Accessed 20 July 2022]

Ward, J. and Marsh, M. (2006) *Sexual Violence Against Women and Girls in War and its Aftermath: Realities, Responses and Required Resources*, Population Fund Briefing Paper [online]. Available from: https://gsdrc.org/document-library/sexual-violence-against-women-and-girls-in-war-and-its-aftermath-realities-responses-and-required-resources [Accessed 20 July 2022]

Webb-Vidal, A. and Frank, M. (2004) 'Venezuela and Cuba trade oil for doctors', *Financial Times* [online]. Available from: www.ft.com/content/12bd92f8-1bae-11d9-8af6-00000e2511c8 [Accessed 20 July 2022]

Welsh, T (2021) 'In Brief: Legal status for Venezuelans in Colombia to improve vaccine access', *devex* [online]. Available from: www.devex.com/news/in-brief-legal-status-for-venezuelans-in-colombia-to-improve-vaccine-access-99118 [Accessed 20 August 2022]

Whelan, A. and Blogg, J. (2007) '"Halfway People": refugee views of reproductive health services', *Global Public Health*, 2: 373–94.

Wickramage, K. and Annunziata, G. (2018) 'Advancing health in migration governance, and migration in health governance', *The Lancet*, 10164: 2528–30.

Wolf, A. (2020) *Just Immigration in the Americas: A Feminist Account*, Lanham, ML: Rowman & Littlefield Publishers.

Women's Refugee Commission (2002) *UNHCR Policy on Refugee Women and Guidelines on their Protection: An Assessment of Ten Years of Implementation* [online]. Available from: www.womensrefugeecommission.org/research-resources/unhcr-policy-on-refugee-women-and-guidelines-on-their-protection-an-assessment-of-ten-years-of-implementation/ [Accessed 15 September 2022]

World Bank (2021) *Venezuela Country Overview* [online]. Available from: www.worldbank.org/en/country/venezuela/overview [Accessed 7 July 2022]

World Health Organization (WHO) (2003) *International Migration, Health & Human Rights* [online]. Available from: https://apps.who.int/iris/bitstream/handle/10665/42793/9241562536.pdf [Accessed 7 July 2021]

WHO (2008) *The Right to Health*, Fact Sheet 31 [online]. Available from: www.ohchr.org/sites/default/files/Documents/Publications/Factsheet31.pdf [Accessed 7 July 2021]

Yamin, A.E. (2016) *Power, Suffering, and the Struggle for Dignity: Human Rights Frameworks for Health and Why They Matter*. Philadelphia, PA: University of Pennsylvania Press.

Zambrano-Barragán, P., Ramírez Hernández, S., Feline Freier, L., Luzes, M., Sobczyk, R., Rodríguez, A. and Beach, C. (2021) 'The impact of COVID-19 on Venezuelan migrants' access to health: a qualitative study in Colombian and Peruvian cities', *Journal of Migration and Health*, 3 [online]. Available from: https://doi.org/10.1016/j.jmh.2020.100029 [Accessed 7 July 2022]

Zapata, G. and Tapia Wenderoth, V. (2021) 'Progressive legislation but lukewarm policies: the Brazilian response to Venezuelan displacement', *International Migration*, 60(1): 132–51.

Zapata, G.P. and Prieto Rosas, V. (2020) 'Structural and contingent inequalities: the impact of Covid-19 on migrant and refugee populations in South America', *Bulletin of Latin America Research*, 39: 16–22 [online]. Available from: https://onlinelibrary.wiley.com/doi/10.1111/blar.13181[Accessed 7 July 2022]

Zetter, R. (2007) 'More labels, fewer refugees: remaking the refugee label in an era of globalization', *Journal of Refugee Studies*, 20 (2): 172–92.

Zuccarelli, G. (2022) 'Female refugee and asylum seekers, and gender injustice: the "effacement", a new face of oppression', PhD Dissertation, University of Milan.

Index

References to figures appear in *italic* type; those in **bold** type refer to tables. References to endnotes show both the page number and the note number (160n5).

D

N

O

V

W

X

Y

Z